# Shield Over Spear

7 Indestructible Principles Of
Success For Leadership
At All Levels

K.D. Wilson

Copyright © 2019 by K.D. Wilson

All rights reserved. No part of this publication may be reproduced, distributed, or transmitted in any form or by any means, including photocopying, recording, or other electronic or mechanical methods, without the prior written permission of the publisher, except in the case of brief quotations embodied in critical reviews and certain other noncommercial uses permitted by copyright law. For permission requests, write to the publisher, addressed "Attention: Permissions Coordinator," at the address below.

Ordering Information:

Quantity sales. Special discounts are available on quantity purchases by schools, college/universities, educators, and others. For details, contact K.D. Wilson at the below address:

**KD@Iamkdwilson.com**

Printed in the United States of America

# Table of Content

| | |
|---|---|
| Note To The Reader | 1 |
| The Beginning | 4 |
| Principle 1: Purpose | 25 |
| Principle 2: Vision | 55 |
| Principle 3: Commitment | 71 |
| Principle 4: Ownership | 93 |
| Principle 5: Strategy | 119 |
| Principle 6: Action | 136 |
| Principle 7: Results | 151 |
| The Finish | 163 |
| Closing Note | 166 |

# Note To The Reader

Tomorrow isn't promised...your time is now! Excuses will only set you back even further, they will never set you free. Once you get that truth into your mind, you can begin. Begin what? Begin life! That's right, until you are living a life of pursuit, faith and truth...are you really living at all? The world needs great leaders, not phenomenal fakes. So, will you rise from the gray and step into the present with hope, heart, and purpose? If so, I believe you just might be fit to lead!

This book is for any person that currently holds, desires, or could possibly see themselves in any position or capacity of leadership. My hope is that no matter where you are in your life, you will consider this book as having been written specifically for you. If so, what that tells me is that you see value in yourself. Though life may have knocked you down at times, as it has us all, you are still here. At the least, you can help lead others up from the places that you've been to and through.

Don't shy away from having the mindset of a leader because of the responsibilities it entails, unless you simply refuse to be accountable and responsible. Be true to yourself, but don't discount yourself, if that makes sense. My prayer is that at the conclusion of this book, you will better understand the responsibility, and power that I know God has placed within us all. No matter who you are, listen to what I'm about to say! You were created with a purpose in mind. You are not an accident. I believe that you too, can lead, because leadership starts with one's self. Shield Over Spear is about building, not breaking.

This book has been intentionally broken down into chapters with several subsections within them. Most, if not all subsections will be labeled with the type of message that correlates with the heading. Don't judge the content by the heading though. Take your time and digest what is being delivered. One subsection is labeled, "Free Game". While this phrase is popular within the cultural boundaries of the African American community primarily; I borrowed it from an entrepreneurial branding genius, and brother of mine named Mahdi Woodard. Google him! Mahdi is, as some may say, 'always dropping free game'. Which is interpreted to mean that he is giving away valuable information that will ultimately prove to be beneficial for those putting his principles to work, at little or no cost. So, enjoy your "Free Game", on me!

You'll notice that as you keep reading the book, the length of the chapters will decrease. I didn't run out of content, this was intentional. The more you learn, the more you should be doing. I wrote this book in such a way that almost all of the principles can be implemented immediately. If you find yourself just consuming, with no output, then you're failing. As the lengths of each chapter thins, your mind and movements should be taking over. Think of it like this...more work and less talk!

The goal of this book is to help you see the power that you have as a person, and leader. I want you to see that your job, as an intern, parent, employee, boss, or student, is to be the best that you can be for yourself, and your team. I guarantee you this, as one that has operated in multiple positions in leadership, there is nothing a team will not do for a great leader. The goal here is not manipulation, its multiplication. I want you to duplicate your greatness once discovered, and cast aside your shortcomings, while helping others avoid those pitfalls. I want you to adopt this formula for leadership success, and add it to your collection of weapons in order to face life's challenges head on. You know how to attack. I want you to begin crushing your opposition with the heaviest weapon you have...the shield.

# THE MAKING OF AN INDESTRUCTIBLE SHIELD

These are the principle elements that form the shield of leadership. I chose to utilize these principles because they work for everyone. Principles don't care about socioeconomic status, race, gender, education, family background, political affiliation, or the likes. Principles flat out work, if you work with them. There is no excuse for you not to increase your leadership ability, attitude, focus, and production if you dedicate yourself to the mastery of these shield creating principles!

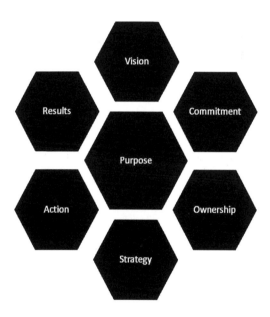

PURPOSE, VISION, COMMITMENT, OWNERSHIP, STRATEGY, ACTION and RESULTS!

These elements on their own are strong, but united, in the hands of a leader they are practically...INDESTRUCTIBLE!

# The Beginning

Rocks began to rattle as the ground vibrated beneath their feet. "Earthquake," the captain said. "No, battle formations," the king responded. As the enemy's army closed in, the king boldly declared... "This is where we hold them! This is where we fight! This...is where they die!" as he looked back at the mighty Spartan warriors. The captain echoed the welcoming love of battle in saying something that still causes my adrenaline to spike every time I hear it. The captain turned to his brothers in arms and roared, "Earn these SHIELDS boys!" Shields, he said. Earn them, he stated. As if they didn't have them in their possession already. I knew what he meant right away. You see, men could talk like a Spartan, dress like a Spartan, and act like a Spartan, but there was one thing that authenticated their identity. That thing, was the shield.

This reference, of an audacious king leading his warriors into battle was birthed from a relatively true story turned movie. This movie was unleashed on the masses in 2007, the year after I finished my times as an undergrad. The movie starring the Scottish actor, Gerard Butler was called, "300." If you haven't seen the movie by now, I don't know what universe you've been visiting because you are behind. It's gory, gruesome, bloody and graphic, but 'My Goodness' is it packed with leadership, and at times, the lack thereof.

In the movie, a Persian representative comes forward and shouts for the Spartans to put down their weapons. To which the defiant king bellowed back, "Come and get them!" What an invitation to fight. What a statement to make. What confidence. What trust! What leadership! You see, the day you become a leader is the day that you stop settling and say, "Enough is enough! Bring it!" As long as you lay down your life at the will and command of others, or obstacles...you will always be a slave. You don't like that do you? Being called a slave? I'd say that I care, but I don't. I'll tell you why. I'm not a jerk, it's just that if you fall into that category...you are your own slave master. We are most often victims of our victim mentality. If you are going to lead, you can't afford to live in yesterday's mistakes and tomorrow's fears. You literally become a mental captive to distress. Your response to life will dictate whether you're a leader, or just a pretty good manager.

The difference in leadership and management, is that one reacts while the other responds. Reaction is initiated through panic and lack of preparation. Managers freak out when the unexpected occurs. Leadership demands response. That just means that whatever happened was expected. Heck, the unexpected is expected. When you know that you must prepare yourself to stay balanced on the waves of life, you'll set yourself up to respond and not react. With a mindset like that, any leader and team can now become enabled to put their pre-planned strategy to work.

"Give them nothing, but take from them...everything!" Leonidas shouted! With a smirk of violent anticipation on his face, shoulders bracing for the impact of his enemy, and eyes fixed on which one he would strike down first, he waited. The valiant leader and king, alongside his brothers, his countrymen, his warriors...waited. Stones trembled and the ground quivered, as the opposing army of more than 100,000 descended all the more on the Spartan military. "Steady" the captain shouted. The overwhelming stampede of rival attackers began to run full speed.

They came yelling at the top of their lungs and with two main weapons swinging in the air recklessly...SWORD and SPEAR!

Big mistake! A few had shields, but not many. And then, like a freight train colliding with an explosive divider, the outcry of weapons clashing sounded off. As thousands of minimally trained Persian men attempted to break through the impenetrable barricade of the king and his mighty warriors, they met two things immediately...SHIELD and SPEAR!

"Push!" the Spartan men belted out! It was at that time, the tables turned, the dust from the king's feet lifted into the air as he and his courageous soldiers transitioned from a successful defense to a horrifically dominant offense. Shield and Spear...Shield and Spear, is all the opposition encountered. The hostiles responded again, with sword and spear, to no avail. With every attempt to retaliate and answer to the Greek's battle tactics, they found themselves retreating further and further back. With every swing at the king or his brothers, there came a shield from multiple angles. They simply could do no major harm to these outnumbered Greek fighters. Within minutes, the mighty king and his combat hardened countrymen were stepping over the fallen enemy opposition. "No prisoners" the captain screamed. "No mercy!" the battle-ready king followed in uproar. "No Spartan dies today!" they declared, and they accomplished just that, with two things in this order, SHIELD and SPEAR!"

What about you though? Do you operate with that same level of passion and fight when it comes to your personal development, and the development of your team? Do you yell out, "No Prisoners...No Mercy?" Maybe you don't yell it, but many of you act like it, and in the wrong way. I don't want you to show disregard for your team, I want you to show no mercy to your average way of thinking. Are you showing no mercy to your poor performance, poor example, and sluggish response? If so, good on you. If not, cut the dead weight, and get on the move.

That is what leadership from any approach truly looks like in the end... achieving the goal, or accomplishing the mission. You cannot accomplish anything by aimlessly attacking, you must be prepared for the situation to change, and in a position to not only guard yourself, but as a leader, to guard others. When a team, of any sorts, is fully aware that the person in charge has their best interest at heart, they will swear their allegiance to them. When a student is certain of the professor's intentions to make them a better scholar, they will follow their instructions. When a CEO puts the well-being of his/her team just beneath the interest of the company's mission, the employees will work on their off days to accomplish the goals of the company with no complaints.

Why? We all want to know that we are cared for, appreciated, loved, valued, and have something to add. I don't care if you're a custodian at a public elementary school, or a U.S. Marine fighting overseas; you need to know that your life matters in the equation. If not, people will respect the power and authority of the one in charge, but they will never respect the person. It's the SHIELD that's the heaviest for a reason, because it has to withstand the most damage. Not just for the one holding it, but also for those it covers.

This leads us into the heart of the book title, "Shield Over Spear!" Before the madness begins to rage, there is a part in the movie "300", that really demonstrates the critical necessity of the shield. In one of the early scenes, a hunchback named Ephialtes (Ef-ee-al-tees) enters the picture. Ephialtes is a rougher version of your childhood Disney character, The Hunchback of Notre Dame...revisited on street level steroids! It's not something I approve of, but in the movie, it was the custom of the Spartan people to only allow children without deformity to live, and most of all, to fight. Ephialtes was the son of a former spartan warrior. His mother, fearing for his life, hid him upon birth. All he wanted was to defend his family name, and prove that he too could be a mighty warrior for his family and country. So, in the movie, from a distance, he followed the king's army.

When things had settled, he presented himself to join the ranks. Ephialtes wore the clothing and armor that his father had earned, and I'm assuming, died in. His spear was perfectly sharpened, and shield pierced with holes from previous battles. When the captain saw him, he turned his blade on him, and called him a monster. Not the king though, he saw a man. Great leaders see the best in people, even when they don't look the part. He asked the king if he could join his warriors to fight the Persians. The king then proceeded to explain the one tactical system that was the source of the Spartan might. It was called, the 'Phalanx.' The 'Phalanx' operated like one fluid turtle shell made of individual soldiers and their shields. When they wanted to strike, they moved the shield, thrusted forward and covered up again. This battle method made it nearly impossible for their opponents to attack them with sword, arrow or spear.

The mighty king stood to his feet and asked Ephialtes to lift his shield as high as he could. It was only a matter of feet off the ground, with very little strength in his carrying arm that allowed him to do so. The king took the next minute and broke down the power of the Phalanx. That being, the tactical ability to use each soldier's shield to cover and move during attack. Every man in the Phalanx protects the man to his left, not himself. It was so critical to be in perfect position that left-handed men were not permitted to serve as soldiers, because the shield must be on the left arm, and sword or spear in the right hand. Did you hear that? The shield they carried, wasn't for them, unless it was close quarters fighting. Leonidas explained to Ephialtes that each man guards the life of the man next to him from his thigh to his neck. Which makes sense, because from the thigh to the neck exists all of your main arteries, organs and major parts of your body.

Like those coming into your business, school, group, or team, they need to know that they will be protected, and their vital organs covered. That doesn't mean that your team should wear their feelings on their sleeves, exposed to the elements. What I'm saying on the other hand is that you should help them guard what's valuable to them, and not rip it away.

So, when family problems show up, you give advice and you cover. When health issues come about, you locate resources for their improvement, and you cover. When someone falls short while displaying a sincere and apologetic heart, you remember all the times that you screwed up, and you cover. Most people don't know what it feels like to have a supervisor or leader protect them from the scorching heat of their situation. They have no clue how it feels to know that the person to their right, and left have their very best interest at heart, and they would sacrifice their comfort just so that they could go on.

What if everybody thought that way on your team? What if everyone walked in ready to do their part, and protect the ones they work with every day? What kind of unstoppable, unified and productive squad would you be a part of if you didn't have to wonder about someone's motives? What if you didn't have to watch your back, or live in fear that one day you'd get an undeserved layoff or separation notice? How would you feel if you knew that you didn't have to fight alone anymore?

Take a second and answer the following question. What would life be like if you worked for, or worked with a genuine person that had your best interests at heart, and would protect you from unnecessary problems?

_____
_____
_____
_____
_____

That is what I want you to do when you finish, and as you progress through this book. I want you to develop a Phalanx system where you guard others, and they guard you. That's not a free-for-all do as you please type of deal. I'm not talking about pacifying unproductive people, instead, I'm asking you to shield them while they sharpen their skills when undeserving situations arise. That goes from the top of the chain of command to the most junior contributor to your team, no matter how far down that may be. When accomplished, or implemented...I guarantee small victories until the major victory is won!

## Who Am I To Tell You About Leadership?

As a former police officer of almost 8 years in the third largest city in North Carolina, I realized that life itself was about purpose, faith, ownership, empathy, and action. But, before action could take place, a decision had to be made. This book is not about me, nor all of my experiences working on the front lines of domestic issues in this country. This book is about leadership, and how it is very much a choice. That's right, leadership is a choice.

I'll never forget the day we graduated from the police academy. It was a momentous occasion because we had just finished almost 6 months of rigorous training. During the graduation ceremony, awards were given out to those recruits exemplifying characteristics of leadership and vast improvement throughout our time of training. I was blessed and fortunate enough to have received 3 of the 6 possible awards given to recruits. I was given the S.C.A.T. Award (Subject Control and Arrest Techniques), P.T. Award (Physical Training), and the highest award a recruit can receive, the Winslow Award. The Winslow Award is an absolute honor, because it is in memory of fallen Officer Michael G. Winslow, who passed in June of 1978. Officer Winslow was responding to assist a fellow officer that needed help. To our understanding, at some point, Officer Winslow lost control of his police vehicle and struck a bridge support, thereby killing him. But, as said before, it wasn't a matter of how he died...it was how he lived that mattered most.

The award, for years on end, has been presented by direct representatives of Officer Winslow's family, often his parents, and if not mistaken, siblings as well. You only received that award if you represented what an officer should be: honorable, coachable, honest, loving, brave, sacrificial and willing to stand in for others. The most humbling part about being the recipient of this award is that like the other recipients of every graduating class, we were selected by our peers. That speaks volumes, because you can't work for that. It's hard to manipulate that selecting process. I could out train everybody and win the fitness award, or study tactics to be the best at arrest techniques, but I, nor others, could trick our entire class into believing that we were great leaders of some sort without them having seen it for some span of time.

When my name was called, I was short of words. I glanced around at my graduating classmates and they all smiled and clapped as if they knew something that I didn't, and in that moment, they did. See, I had voted for a friend of mine, someone that I looked up to everyday in the academy. Ironically, he had voted for me. But that's what leaders should do, right? They should always find, and pull out the best in others. If I could've voted for myself, I still wouldn't have. I knew all of my mess, and how much I needed to grow. Funny though isn't it? We look at our poor qualities first, and seldomly appreciate the things we do right. We infrequently take a second to celebrate the good things and habits that we pursue daily. Change that!

Though I did not choose to work toward becoming a high-ranking officer, I, like every officer, was forced and expected to lead in some way all the time. When you were in route and dispatched to a disturbance, car crash, house fire, narcotics issue, and even homicide...you were expected to lead. But leadership was not just the ability to perform a task, it was an overall presence of the individual. My former Sergeant used to say, "You stand for more than yourself now. Your leadership role doesn't take place on scene, it takes place in your mind and before you even exit your patrol car." What he was saying was easy for me to understand. It would've been wrong for me to get out of the car looking sloppy, disheveled, spaced out and thrown off, only to see an issue and attempt to assert myself as a person in control. How are you going to control a situation when you're not even taking time to control yourself first?

Maybe some of you are struggling in your leadership role because you've lacked the discipline of personal accountability. You only step up when it's your turn to hold somebody else accountable for their actions. That's even a biblical No-No! The bible says, get the beam out of your own eye before telling somebody to get the splinter out of theirs.

So, I took my appearance, mindset, and even my internal

attitude serious every day. In the policing profession, at least in the city I served, we operated under two titles on dispatched calls. You had primary, and you had secondary/assist. If you wanted to be a good friend and take a traffic crash or fill out a report for a buddy, before you could even take over her/his role, you had to acknowledge acceptance of the task. You had to physically go on to your personal police computer screen and hit a button that read, "Primary Unit". Isn't that something? That's why I say that leadership is a lifestyle and a choice. Someone can force you into a position, but they can't make you be your best and own the situation. If you don't make a conscious decision to grow up and operate under a standard greater than average, you can expect to be a lackluster follower all of your life.

Two major keys to being a fair and effective officer was communication and respect. If you could master those two things, 8/10 times you could probably achieve a desired result. Again, leadership is about understanding self, the mission, the situation, and others. The officers that struggled the most, and ended up with the highest use of force incidents were typically those that had a chip on their shoulder. They talked to people however they felt, or in light of the incident, and they often treated them as if they were "other" or "less than." It's no wonder those were also the officers screaming on the radio like a wounded chihuahua asking for help. They applied spear first, only intending to use their shield for themselves. Their shield would have been patience, fueled by understanding. Their shield would have been discretion in the place of black and white rules. Their shield would have simply been decent humanity.

Effective officers would arrive on scene, and when possible, use respectful terms such as 'sir' or 'maam/miss.' This simple tactical move shields the person from their TV assumptions that all officers are militant and overbearing. To a small degree it has the power to decrease implicit bias on both sides. It's still SHIELD OVER SPEAR, and good leadership.

As one that wore a uniform, and answered over 6,000 dispatched calls over a span of almost 8 years, I learned just as much from my mistakes as I did from the things I got right the first time. I had great supervisors that were shining examples of leaders, and I had crappy individuals that were just given more rank and authority because they were friends with somebody or they took written promotional tests well. What I'm saying is, I could tell a leader when I was around one because they built you up and made you better. They operated with a shield in hand and a sword in the other, but you knew the sword would never be turned on you. That level of safety, bond, and for me, brotherhood, was something I'll always cherish.

War is either about power, or it's about freedom. Occasionally, it's about both, but it's definitely about opposition, it's about allegiance and dedication, even unto death. Dedication to what though? Allegiance to who, you may be asking? That's simple. To something bigger than oneself. On that battlefield of selflessness, leaders step forward out of the muck and mire. Warriors launch counter attacks towards their opposition with hearts full of love for one another, and something I've already mentioned...the Mission.

In the movie, before king Leonidas led his 300 soldiers into battle against the invading Persian army led by the dictator Xerxes, his wife and son met him outside of the city walls. She called out, "Spartan!" He turned and responded, "Yes my lady?" Then she said something that shook me to the core. She gazed into his very being and said, "Come back with your shield, or on it!" She knew that he was about to face seemingly insurmountable odds, and enemy numbers like never before. She knew that he would give all of his energy and focus to that which waited for him miles ahead. She knew that he would defeat a tremendous number of adversaries. And most of all, she knew that there was a strong chance she would never see him again. Yet, she did not attempt to restrain or persuade him. What kind of a wife was she? Knowing that her son may be fatherless in a matter of days, what was she thinking? She wasn't thinking at all; she didn't have to.

She knew that she didn't marry a man in authority alone, she married a sacrificial leader. One that would give his last breath to prevent others from having to give theirs. One that would not order from the rear, but lead the charge himself. She knew, and in knowing and responding the way she did, she too exemplified leadership. It takes a special kind of woman to notice such a thing. You see, in the ancient Greek culture, particularly for soldiers, your shield was practically sacred. You could break a sword, snap a spear, and even lose a piece of your armor. But, you never, ever, lost or surrendered your shield.

What does this have to do with leadership, you may be wondering? Let's look a bit further. She didn't tell him to come back with his sword, spear, or even to come back with all of his soldiers. No, she said, "Come back with your shield, or on it!" It was the custom of the Spartans to bring their fallen leaders back home resting on their shields if they could not carry it themselves. It was a sign of honor, that they fought fiercely until the very end, and protected those they loved. That is what leadership is about, your ability to protect, guard and help others, while completing the mission set before you. I am not implying that the mission is to appease subordinates and those working under you, not at all.

I am saying that you have to understand the power of teamwork as it relates to accomplishing a desired end or goal. The people assigned to your upkeep should be taken care of so that they can take care of the mission. If an individual is neglected, mistreated or abused for too long, they will spend more time guarding themselves and less time focusing on the task at hand. In that case, punishment will only go so far. The pain of punishment will never mount up to the pain of giving in to a person that mistreats and disrespects you. With this being true, they'll take that day off, that zero on an assignment, and that minimal pay cut if it saves their dignity and allows them to get away from you. The purpose is not to damage morale, sow discord, and punish for lack of performance on demand. It is to challenge and empower instead!

When we think of the word, "Leadership", we often use words such as: strong, courageous, bold, direct, loyal, trustworthy, relentless, sharp, consistent, and unafraid. While there may be some credit given to individuals that possess some of these qualities, a leader is much more than a few summed up catch phrases. Leadership is not just hopeful positivity; leadership is action and follow through. Let's not forget, leaders have everything and nothing to prove at the same time. They must demonstrate their ability to usher others into progressive victory, while holding true to their own standards. Likewise, they must have skin tough enough to defend against enemy attack. This can be an attack on their integrity, finances, internal conversation, or their very lives.

Either way, it's a fight that every leader must face and win consistently. They can't be so concerned about what others think that they become a puppet to their situations and circumstances. On the other hand, they can't ignore their people so much that their subordinates struggle to find direction under their command. If we're honest with ourselves, we follow leaders because of their potential ability to make us better, and complete the shared mission. We see their many accomplishments, demeanor under pressure, and decision-making ability and that attracts us like moths to a flame.

That's why I often say that leaders can manage, but few managers can truly lead. So, with that in mind, I have a question. Are you a leader? If so, why, and how did you become one? What makes you what you say you are, and most of all, will anybody attest to it other than you? If not...why not, and what's the hold up? What is it that's keeping you from stepping into a role that embodies progress?

_____

_____

_____

_____

_____

_____

Those are simple questions that many fail to ask themselves and only apply to others. That's because most people associate leadership with telling people what to do. While there is a component associated with delegation, that is not what a leader is at all. It takes more than your ability to place others in positions to meet a deadline, to be a real leader. The late Mahatma Ghandi challenged us with this familiar charge, "Be the change you want to see in the world." If you're wondering what that has to do with leadership, I'm not wondering why you're reading this book. Leadership is about example, not just explanation. Anybody can tell you what they want done. My two-year-old boy tells me all the time that he wants to play, desires a snack, or has to poop. Too much information? Sorry, ha-ha. Just because he tells me what he wants, and attempts to tell me what to do, notice the "attempt" part, that doesn't make him the leader of the house.

No more does it make any person a leader that simply belts out what they want accomplished without stepping in to provide vision, clarity, model and purpose for others first. The late Bishop Otis Lockett Sr. used to say, "Just because you live in a garage, that doesn't make you a car." Likewise, being in a position of leadership doesn't make you a leader. Leadership is something that companies hire and fire for. It's what colleges, and universities look for as qualities attained by their incoming and outgoing students. It's what spouses look for in their significant others. Leadership is not a soft, and cozy word, it's a kick in the face. A good kick though. Leadership, broken down by denotation actually tells on itself. It encompasses two obvious words, 'Leader', and 'Ship'. So, let's look at that for just a minute before we really dig in and I start asking all the hard questions that you'll hate me and love me for later.

"Leader," in general terms can be defined as the person in command, the principal element of a party, the conductor, or driving force. A "Ship," on the other hand, is just as easily described. The word 'ship' means, support, vessel, and even aircraft. What's the center piece of a ship though? It's ability to carry weight. That's right, if you consider yourself to be a leader, you have to be able to carry more than your own share. That doesn't mean that you cripple other people by spoon feeding them or never allowing anyone else to make a decision. That's not leadership, those sound like control and balance issues. You have to know what's profitable for all and what's not.

For instance, relationship is key when it comes to long standing leadership, in my opinion. A person in leadership can't be too far removed from those they are over. If they are, resentment due to dislocation to task and reality upon assignment will surely set in. This goes for a college student over a group project, an assembly line supervisor at a plant, or bank manager, and the likes. True leaders don't just order their subordinates around, they develop relationship with them, and they listen to them. To neglect the fact that God gave us two ears and one mouth, for a leader in authority, it could prove to be catastrophic, and in some cases, even fatal. Allow me to share a story with you that encompasses the epitome of great leadership from an unranked warrior, and horrendous failure to listen, lead, and act in combat by a ranking official.

## Leadership Needs No Title

There is an incident that took place mid-year of 2009 in Afghanistan between U.S. armed forces and terrorist insurgents. From what has been gathered, a meeting with local elders and leaders was scheduled to take place. This meeting would prove to be an opportunity for peace in particular areas of the country. As U.S. troops were transported in for the meeting, shots rang out from AK-47 assault rifles all around them. It was a set up! The U.S. soldiers were out of reach, and barely able to return fire due to the overwhelming firepower of the radical attackers. It is said that the soldiers radioed in to the nearest base for assistance. "We need an evacuation right now!" the soldier said. "Negative...it's too hot, we can't risk a bird (helicopter) going down." the commander replied. "We are under heavy fire, and we need help now!" the soldier responded. "We'll send help as soon as we can, just wait 15 minutes." he told the soldier.

The coward terrorist attackers began to close the distance on the four U.S. soldiers pinned down in the middle of a brutal gunfight. Not far off were a group of U.S. Marines. One particular Marine realized that U.S. troops were pinned down, and radioed in for air assistance, or even support from gunships near the coast. To his surprise, he got the same response, "Negative! Wait 15 minutes." The Marine couldn't believe it as he recalled the horrible day, and stated that 15 minutes turned into 30 minutes and then 45 minutes and still, there was no help.

The overwhelmed U.S. soldiers were running out of time and ammunition. They were outgunned and outnumbered on all sides. Once more, the soldier, after having been set up and with bullets whizzing past his face radioed in for aerial assistance to the nearby base. And, once again, he was told to wait. He then reportedly told the commander, "If you don't send us help...we are going to die!" But help didn't come from over the phone, it came from a U.S. Marine willing to disregard orders to standby.

The Marine grabbed another soldier and told him, "We are going in!" The two soldiers grabbed an unarmored truck nearby. The primary Marine slung a high-powered weapon over the top, standing in the bed as the other soldier drove straight towards the pinned down troops. The Marine recalled the incident and said, "I knew I was going to die, but if I did, I would die trying to save my brothers." And into the fire they went, bullets now whizzing past their faces and piercing the unarmored domestically driven pickup truck. With hearts beating through their chests and adrenaline spiked through the roof of their bodies, they moved closer and closer. The soldier driving told reporters that he remembered bullets coming in the passenger window, inches from his face and out of the driver side window at speeds that only tracer fire (light) could show. The Marine on the gun tagged as many as he could, desperately trying to reach the soldiers that he could no longer see hunkered down, waiting for a miracle. The Marine then realized the truck had gone as far as it would go, and he jumped out of the back and took off on foot.

He said in an interview, he remembered running for what felt like the longest run of his life. All he wanted to do was get to the troops. As he neared their location, he dove into a ditch to seek cover until he could formulate his next plan. He then advised that he didn't hit the ground as expected. No, he didn't hit the ground at all. He landed on the soldier that he last heard calling for help on the radio. The soldier that had just warned the commander, the supervisor safe back on base, that they needed help. The soldier that was told to wait for 15 minutes almost three times. The soldier whose deceased body broke the fall of the Marine trying to save him.

The Marine then realized that all four courageous U.S. armed forces warriors had passed away due to enemy fire. The Marine did make it out safely, as helicopters finally flew in even though they were denied permission to assist. It was over an hour that they waited, and in that hour, because of the lack of leadership, and poor decision making on the part of the commander, U.S. troops died. The commanding officer surrendered his shield to his emotions instead of using his authority to save those that were only there to save and fight for others.

That's where poor listening becomes fatal, when we only hear from our place of complacency and safety. When the sense of urgency only relates to what we can get out of the equation, you fail. If that commander had been on the scene, he would have responded differently I'm sure, but his distance awarded him the opportunity to think. An opportunity that came down to microseconds for those amazing U.S. troops fighting terrorist insurgents. That was the opposite of leadership!

The Marine and his teammate on the other hand, exemplified the epitome of leadership down to their willingness to shield others from death, even if it meant giving their own lives. Leadership that wasn't a second guess issue, but simply taking inventory of the situation and realizing that someone needed a shield and a spear at their side. So, instead of looking around for help, and waiting for a green light, those two soldiers became the help. They issued their own green light!

It's people like that, the ones willing to go the distance, not just for themselves, but for others, that make things work. Do you know what the root meaning of the word 'passion' is? Passion translates to 'suffering,' so I ask...what are you willing to suffer for? It's Harriet Tubman, Dr. Martin Luther King, Mother Teresa, Nelson Mandela and the likes, that were living examples of leadership and passion walked out. Those willing to disregard social norms in order to establish equality. That is the lifeblood of leadership. It is the "Yes" of the heart, under fire from the, "No!" It's relationship that made the difference.

But a leader can't get too close either. If a leader has no boundaries, this could prove to be disastrous. When team members get too close to the leader, they begin to internally take on unassigned authority themselves. If one feels like their boss is their best friend forever, which is fine with limitations, they may assume that their relationship offers them perks that others may not get. Loss of respect, tenure dismissed, requests overlooked and so much more can happen. There has to be a balance where the leader knows his/her team intimately, but is still able to take charge and dominate the scene when need be.

What I want you to know is that you have the ability to lead at whatever level you are currently at. Let me repeat that because 99% of the human race misses this point. You can lead from any position! If you're a mechanic, you can lead. If you're a pilot, you can lead. If you're a dog-on bee keeper, you can lead. If you're the pastor, or retail sales associate, you can lead. Leadership isn't about a title, it's about influence and tenacity. You can be a leader, but you must understand first, what a leader is, and what it is not.

You have to grasp the brutal reality that positional leadership is not for everyone, even though I believe that every human has the capacity to lead. What I mean by positional leadership, is one appointed to operate within a certain role. This may be easier to understand in context of sports, business and education. There has to be a coach for a sports team, but every player and staff member still has the capacity to lead also. The difference is that whoever is ultimately in charge of all, is responsible for all. It's the nature of their position. So, no matter where you find yourself in life right now, or even the shortcomings, regrets, and challenges of your yesterday...you're still alive, and there's time to apply pressure to your fears, doubts and disbelief. I'm going to show you how to utilize the internal weaponry of true leaders. I'm going to introduce you to my "Indestructible 7!" The seven things I've seen placed at the top of the list for all high performing leaders.

This is what took me from a "D" average in high school, and graduating in the bottom percentile of my high school class to graduating in the top percentile of my master's program at Duke University. That 3.74 G.P.A. may not be much to some of you, but I did it while working full time as a patrol officer. Try figuring out hermeneutics and finishing a robbery report at the same time. I did my grad school homework backed into dark parking lots on Microsoft Word in between calls at 4 a.m. I commuted an hour each way three days a week and still won. So yeah, when I say they're indestructible...I mean it!

## Here's my Indestructible 7 :

1. Purpose
2. Vision
3. Commitment
4. Ownership
5. Strategy
6. Action
7. Results

Treat these principles like weapons. A sword in the hand of a master swordsman can help you win the war. A sword in the hands of a coward does no good. In the same way, you have to apply these simple principles skillfully. If you think these principles are too rudimentary, I'd say give them a try in everything you do before solidifying your criticism into your psychology. These have been tested and proven, and if you take them out of order, you're going to screw some stuff up. I'm just asking you to trust me for a minute, and if you don't like how things are turning out at the end...go back to what doesn't work. (Insert Smiley Sarcastic Face Here)

I believe in being equipped for the challenge ahead. So, I'll share one of my favorite stories with you:

*One day, a pupil asked his master a question. He said, "Master, you have always taught me to live a life of peace. Yet, every day you train with your sword like a man prepared for battle." The grandmaster leaned over at his pupil and smiled. Then he replied, "My son, it is better to be a warrior in a garden of peace, than a gardener in the middle of a brutal war."* In short, leaders are always prepared!

# Principle 1: Purpose

*"When the purpose of a thing is not known, abuse is inevitable!"*

*- Dr. Myles Munroe*

**PURPOSE**, is the reason for which something is done, exists, or was made.

In the opening scenes of the movie "300," the young king is torn away from his mother and thrown into the wilderness to fend for himself. He is exposed to the elements, beaten to a pulp, and left to fight of a ferocious beast that seeks to eat him for dinner. The scene slows a bit, the narration picks up. The young king was calm, luring and prepared, as the starving beast approached. He backed into the mouth of a small cave in the midst of the winter cold. Wearing nothing but a waist cloth, he remained focused as the vicious wolf hybrid snarled and salivated at the thought of his demise.

Then, the wolf lunged forward with midnight fangs exposed ready for the kill. One quick movement was all it took. The young king sent the beast tumbling to the ground. In the next scene, the boy returns a man. This time though, he was dressed in the skin of the monster that tried to consume him. One might think that it was a harsh thing to do, sending a child into the elements. In the end, you see that it was all surrounded by purpose. The young boy had to prove that he was capable of defending his city, people and future family against any force, no matter how grotesque it may be. The winter cold taught him lessons that allowed him to enjoy the summer breeze.

The breakdown of the word, purpose, actually shows that part of its makeup is to display design. Purpose has purpose. That's right, you may not know exactly what you're supposed to be doing in the world, just yet, but you were designed on purpose. There is no way that God overlooked the fact that you are here, and living. The gifts, talents, life experiences and ideas that you have, automatically qualify you to contribute good into the world.

The very first thing one must understand about being a leader, is that you have a choice. The late Dr. Myles Munroe used to teach on the leadership qualities of the lion. He would often speak on the fact that the lion isn't the biggest, baddest, or most brilliant animal in the wild...but he is the king.

And what is it that makes this massive cat such a respected terror in the animal kingdom? It's his belief system. For whatever reason, the lion believes that it's the biggest, baddest mo-fo out there, and it acts like it. The lion, at some point, made a choice to be at the top of the food chain, and it has never been dethroned. The hippo could kill a lion, an elephant, giraffe, or even a crocodile too, but when the lion shows up, these animals back up. It's not to say that lions are invincible, because they're not, but they live what they believe, and that's what makes them a leader.

If you don't check what you're telling yourself every day, you'll always be the victim of self-sabotage. Remember, the most important conversation you'll have every day is the conversation you have with yourself. The mighty rhinoceros is a victim of its own beliefs. The rhino could destroy a lion if it wanted to, but when the cat comes around, they take the detour. Why? They're a product of their belief system. They think the lion can crush them whenever they want, and that they're always in danger. While the lion is a professional hunter, it would take more than one bite to drop a rhino. In the same way, make sure that you're not becoming a victim of your own thoughts when it comes to leadership. Look at the big picture, and know that you have what it takes to walk the walk.

But still, what makes even the belief system valid? It is the mission that breathes life into the mind. Therefore, because you have a mission, you have a purpose. You aren't just trudging forward into nothingness; well you shouldn't be at least. Without a mission, you are like an aimless grenade, full of explosive potential with nowhere to go. The mission, folks, is what matters. There is always a mission or an objective in every single thing you do. I literally mean that, by the way. What's the mission behind your lungs working? To keep oxygen flowing into your body in order for blood to flow properly to your heart and brain, right? Eh, kind of. The mission is to keep you alive! The functionality of the lungs is just the job.

But, here's the interesting part. If asked, which organ is most important? Many would automatically say, "The heart." But, what about the brain, veins, and lungs that help oxygenate the blood that flows to the same heart most deem as the leader of all organs? What now? Are the lungs the most important? If so, what about the nose and mouth? After all, if either of those two are blocked, it limits the intake of oxygen and the lungs are useless. I hope you're understanding what I'm getting at here. Where there is a mission, there is the capacity for leadership at every level.

In the movie, Leonidas was obsessed with protecting Sparta, and for all intents and purposes, Greece as well. Everything that he did was anchored by one word that he was willing to die for...Freedom! Freedom for his country, freedom for his people, and freedom for his wife and son. That was the purpose. That was his mission. Why? Because there are four things that purpose should always do:

1. **Add value to your life, and others.**
2. **Be worth sacrificing for.**
3. **Provide a sense of fulfillment.**
4. **Lead you toward the final destination.**

Because he knew exactly what he was after, there were no boundaries that he was unwilling to cross, and no distance that he was unwilling to stretch out for. Here is the phenomenal piece though, in the movie, before they set off to a place called, "The Hot Gates", an unranked leader makes himself known. As the king inspects the men, one of his select few, Stelios (Side Note: Leaders reproduce leaders!) stepped forward, opening his chest to the air with spear in hand and shield in the other. With grit, violent eyes, a raspy voice and a fully committed heart, he spoke these words, "We are with you sire. For Sparta, for freedom, to the death!" The king acknowledged him with a look of gratitude and a smirk of great expectation. The look of brotherhood. The look of common bond.

I wondered though, where did that come from? What was it about the king that had rallied the hearts of warriors to the point in which they were willing to lay down their lives? The only men allowed to come were soldiers with born sons to carry on their names. They knew what awaited their arrival. Then I listened again to what Stelios said, "We are with you sire. For Sparta, for freedom, to the death!" He let the king know that on behalf of all the men, they knew that he would not have them do something he was not willing to do himself. He said, "We are with YOU!" He didn't say, "Thanks for sending us." Most of all, they rallied behind him because they knew the king was not a selfish man. He lived for something greater than himself. He lived for his country, and he lived for freedom. Those two things he was willing to gladly die for at any time. That's what leaders do though, they embody the mission and purpose to the point that it is never questionable whether or not they are about more than themselves.

What about you? Are you the type of person that honestly seeks personal gain? Do you attempt to wrap up your agenda in the mission so as to make it seem like you're not something that you really are? Have you experienced some kind of hurt that only allows you to stay in defensive mode, protecting yourself from any and all things that might backfire on you? I'll tell you this, people can sense authenticity a mile away, and you can only act but for so long. If you're finding yourself being fake, do yourself a favor...knock it off before it catches up to you. Even if you have to start from the bottom. A true start, living and moving on purpose is better than jumping to the front of the line with a hidden agenda.

Are you the kind of leader that people say, "We will follow you, to the death"? That might mean the death of your career, the death of your education, or your social status. Would people follow you because of the way you project your heart into the world? If that seems far-fetched to you, take a look at history. Martin Luther King Jr. believed in equality and freedom for all, particularly people of color. People lost their jobs following his lead, had their houses burned to the ground, people were literally lynched and hung in trees, and beaten by public officials. Was that not a worthy cause though? Freedom and justice for all? Wasn't Leonidas fighting for the same thing, to a degree, that Dr. King was? What about Nelson Mandela? He was imprisoned for years, and upon his release he was elected as president of South Africa. Why? Was it because he had served time in prison? I think not. No, it was because he embodied the mission that the people cared about. He wanted two things, freedom and justice for his country. Do you see the similarity yet?

If you're going to be an effective and impacting leader, you need to soak in the purpose of whatever you're getting behind. That doesn't matter if you're a class president in college, business CEO, program director, or landscaper. Why do you do what you do? If you can't answer that. You cannot lead! What you will find yourself doing is managing and delegating deadlines to others in order to save face.

Do you know why street gangs are so attractive to young people these days? It's not the money alone, drugs, reckless living or even the violence. No, it's the human desire to 'BELONG!" That's why young people flock to gangs, because it's bigger than one person and there is safety within numbers. It's simultaneously all about the individual member and the whole gang at the same time. Why? The three-musketeer mentality, all for one and one for all. If your team knows that you value something worth fighting for, they will get behind you as long as you demonstrate the qualities of a good person, committed to the cause.

The purpose gives the leader fuel to inspire the masses. But, as stated, when the person in a position of leadership sacrifices the purpose for personal profit, everything falls apart. It must be modeled, not just explained. Leadership must be seen, not dreamed. With that in mind, I want you to answer a few questions for me:

- Who modeled true leadership in your life growing up?

_____

_____

- Do you have any feelings about yourself in light of leadership?

_____

- When have you ever felt like you did a poor job leading? What happened?

- Have you ever felt like you nailed an opportunity as a leader? When/How?

- What's your purpose as a leader?

- If I were a follower, would you be worth following and learning from as you currently are? Why?

- Be honest, are you living a life worth dying for? If not, what the heck are you waiting for?

The questions listed above are all very introspective. I've found that if one is willing to be brutally honest with oneself, they are twice as likely to be honest with others. What comes from honesty is trust, and from trust grows confidence. The confidence I'm speaking of is not just confidence for you, but rather, others developing confidence in the person that you are, and the person you are still becoming. That's the issue though, most people won't be honest, because their pride is in the way of their progress.

Former Navy Seal Commander Jocko Willink said, "Ego is the enemy of every leader, and humility is their greatest asset." Jocko would know, he was a warfare commander overseas! He didn't say it was their ability to create, or be innovative. He never mentioned their hours of educational credits on a subject matter. No, he said that 'humility' was the winning factor. Simply put, humility is a state of being humble. Not esteeming and priding yourself above that which you really are. On the contrary, it also does not mean that you belittle yourself and put your accomplishments down. Let's not forget the example of the human body. The heart can't say to the lungs, "you're worthless". Everything has a purpose and a function.

## *Free Game*

Never base your purpose on the opinion of others, good or bad, because you relinquish ownership of your WHY! Spend less time proving other people wrong, and spend more time proving yourself right! When you do that, you're only working for you.

## **Purpose Doesn't Permit...Procrastination**

I was once lecturing at a major university in Georgia, when I asked the students if any of them were procrastinators. Hands shot up into the air, some were only halfway because they were ashamed to admit it, and a few just blurted out "YUP!" I singled out one of the students and asked, why he procrastinates? The young man raised his head and said, "I'm just lazy I guess". "Hmm" I responded, with my face scrunched up. "Don't believe you!" I told him. He said, "How can you not believe me when I'm telling you that I'm just lazy?" So, I asked him a question. "What if I could cure your procrastination in two minutes would you want me to show you how?" I asked him.

"Of course," he said. "Good man!" I responded. "Let me ask you something, and this is for anybody, if I told you that I could show you how to make a guaranteed 4.0 for the rest of your college experience would you be here in this room at 4:25 AM?" Everyone in the room agreed that they would be in the classroom at the given time. And then I added, "What about 4:25 AM on a Saturday during spring break?" Groaning flowed around the classroom for obvious reasons, but still, a large amount of the class said they would be there. The young man glanced around and smirked as if he had me stumped.

"OK, now I have another question for you. What if I told you that we could talk about shoes in this classroom at 4:25 AM on a Saturday during your spring break, would you be here?" I asked. "Of course not," everybody yelled. I think I even got an expletive roared back. "So, what's the difference," I asked? "Nobody gives a crap about shoes, especially during spring break. But everybody wants to get a great score on their test and GPA," a student blurted out. "Agreed," I said. "But, what's the difference in your response to the two questions on the same date, at the same time, and in the same place?" They said the same again, "It's the 4.0 that matters," I smiled and then glared at the young man that had labeled himself a procrastinator. I replied, "Exactly!

"Do you know why you would not be here for shoes, but you would be here for a great GPA boost? It's because procrastination is directly tied to priority, and priority is married to purpose," I said. Even though I had given them such a great gem, some of them still didn't quite understand. So, I broke it down for them. "Your priority in school is to graduate with the highest GPA possible. Therefore, even during spring break, a time allotted for vacation and relaxation, you value a greater GPA more than time to relax. What you're telling me is that you prioritize progress and achievement over vacations and slumming on the beach. Naturally, you only prioritize that because of the purpose in which you attend school in the first place. And it is not just to simply get a degree."

"Why are you here," I asked. "What do you mean?" the student responded. "It's a simple question really, why are you here?" I asked again with a little bit of a higher pitch in my voice. "I am here to get a degree and learn I guess" the college student responded. And then I said something that threw them all off. "Liar," I said.

They looked at me bewildered, and asked me why I would say such a thing? I asked the young man the question again. "Why are you in school?", now with the rest of the class staring directly at the college freshman. He responded back, "I'm here to get my degree so that I can get a good job after I graduate." I asked, "But why? He responded, "To make money I guess?" "You guess?" I asked. He said "Yeah, that's the goal right, to get a degree and make money and start a family and have a house one day." I asked him, "Are you asking me or telling me?" He said "Well that's why I'm here." I walked out from behind the podium and down the center aisle up the stairs towards him and as I looked into his eyes I said "I don't believe you."

I continued on, "Let me ask you another question then. What are you studying here at the University of Georgia?" "Biology", he said. "Great, I struggled in that during my college days, where the heck were you when I needed you jerk?" I asked, smiling. By then, I could tell I was getting on his nerves, but I had piqued his interest. "So why are you majoring in biology." I questioned. "Because I want to help people", he said. "Good for you", I responded, "But that's not the whole picture. So, why do you want to use biology to help people," I asked. And then the room fell quiet as the tears welled up in his eyes. "My grandmother has cancer, and I've never felt more helpless in my life" he responded with a raspy voice.

With an expression of pride toward him, and sympathy simultaneously written on my face, "That's it my friend," I said! "That's why you're here. With a reason like that, resistance doesn't stand a chance. It's not just to get a degree is it?" "No sir," he responded. "I have to be a doctor and help find a cure to help other people, so that they don't have to experience what my family and I are experiencing right now."

"I'm totally behind you and I love everything about what you just said. Man, I freaking believe in you dude! That's why I was asking the questions over and over. You need to have your purpose in the front of your mind at all times, or else, when trouble comes your way you will forget and quit. This school thing is bigger than getting a piece of paper and a fancy plaque. It's about making a difference in the world, and for you my young friend, it's about making a difference in your own family. That is what leadership is about... Living to create change! So, I better not ever hear you give out that garbage excuse of being lazy or a procrastinator. And that goes for everybody else in the room," I said. I finished out the talk by reminding them that when you have purpose attached to people, passion and pain...You are unstoppable!

Although I believe that he had misdiagnosed his issue, I was proud of the young man for being honest about his lazy mindset. True leaders are able to admit their shortcomings, faults and failures to their team. People are afraid that someone will look down on them and question their qualification though. I've seen the polar opposite happen. Because of their honesty, more times than not, they are celebrated and recognized as authentic by those following them. Relationships can be built on purpose and with the goal in mind if a balanced amount of exposure and truth is present.

Ultimately, if you are in a role of leadership to any degree, you don't have time to lie to yourself or others. Honesty is the cutting tool that creates a key that unlocks the future. Truth chisels away all of the things that keep you hindered. You don't have time to act like you know it all, and like you've got it all together. That's trash leadership. As a matter of fact, it's not leadership at all. Anybody willing and desiring to push others into greatness, must do so by example and intentionality. The purpose of decisions should always be linked to the purpose or mission of the team. Healthy working relationships are part of purpose, if you didn't get the memo.

Simon Sinek is one of my all-time favorite speakers on leadership. As a phenomenal author, and optimist, he said this on a video interview:

*"The great leaders are not the strongest, they are the ones who are honest about their weaknesses.*

*The great leaders are not the smartest; they are the ones who admit how much they don't know.*

*The great leaders can't do everything; they are the ones who look to others to help them.*

*Great leaders don't see themselves as great; they see themselves as human."*

## **Sweets, Books, And Growth**

A leader that fails to understand the purpose of the mission and their role, will always be an ineffective leader. They will ultimately and in some way, cause more harm than good because they are operating with partial blindfolds on. Leadership without direction, in one way or another is pointless. Think of it this way, for you to be a leader you must know where you're going, or at least have an understanding of the current that's moving you forward. If you do not understand 'what,' then the 'why' is insignificant. Sometimes it's vice versa, but you understand what I mean. There is this close friend of mine that I've always considered to be a great leader. Having been in the profession of law-enforcement and policing, leadership is not something that one takes lightly. And within a profession such as that, leadership, or the lack there of, could very well mean life or death.

My friend, Sgt. Rose, I'll call him, had infectious leadership qualities. I remember being on a patrol unit when he came to the division, and took over one of the specialized units that I worked closely with. That particular team had been operating at an average level. Not doing anything out of sorts or wrong, but definitely not setting a standard either, until Sgt. Rose showed up. When I say he showed up, he showed up! Sgt. Rose came in with the mentality that leaders and followers work together to achieve a common goal. Thereby empowering the followers to become leaders themselves.

He did not come in with the mindset that he was going to dominate each individual's attitude, and show them who the boss was. This was not an old Western, where the new authority figure comes in and says "There is a new sheriff in town." Instead, Sergeant Rose came in and got right to work with understanding the layout of the land, asking those that had already been a part of that unit for their input on how the team could become better, and ultimately developing strong relationships that again proved infectious in the best way possible.

Having been a former member of that unit myself, I knew the ups and downs of the job. There were very unique issues that you had to deal with being on that team that other patrol officers did not have to work through on such a consistent basis. Sgt. Rose, as previously stated, came in and immediately told his officers, "Look team, I'm the new guy here, and I need your help. What's working and what's not? Where can we be stronger, and how can we win every day, every shift?" I wasn't even in the room when this introduction really took place. But like a kid getting a new toy, the officers came out of that meeting excited and pumped up as if they were all on the job for the first day themselves. That's what leadership does, it brings new air into old places.

Question, do you bring more smog into the room, or fresh air? Do people hold their breath when you show up, or do they sigh with relief? With the way that you lead those around you, no matter what level you are in, as a student in college, or the CFO of a major company, what element of refreshment do you bring when you enter the room? If you cannot say that you bring life to the room, then you are automatically bringing death. Meaning, if you are not increasing the productivity, progress, and empowerment of others, then you are holding them at the same average standard, or pushing them down. Both are equally destructive.

I remember leaving my line up one morning, and Sgt. Rose was just starting his lineup with the unit that he was newly over. Being that he was my friend, I stepped in to say hello, and I was welcomed as if I were a part of the team myself. He told me to sit down, and I did. He then asked two of the most seemingly random questions I had ever heard in all of my years of policing. He asked all the men in the room if we would prefer chocolate cake or apple pie, and why? And then, he asked what books we were currently reading? I laughed at first, but I failed to see that he was establishing a relationship, and breaking up the monotony of the normal routine lineups that every officer had come to dread. We all knew that we had to meet in the mornings or before our shift started to get the rundown of our day and what particular issues needed to be addressed in the city, and particularly in our respective work zones.

Some supervisors were great at bringing fresh air into the room as I previously stated. They keep things light and intentional when it comes to the job, and don't put their squads in position to fail. I unfortunately would say that 60% of supervisors come in with a mono tone voice or a demanding facial expression and simply report what the chief or captains of the divisions mandate that we get done. Nobody likes being thrown tasks from above without understanding the significance, or at bare minimum feeling as if what we were doing was appreciated.

But that was the normal layout of most lineups. Walk in on time, sit down, shut up, listen, and go to work. That sucked. Sgt. Rose never had a boring lineup. And because of his ability to bring fresh air into the room every day, no matter his own personal struggles that he had in his own life, officers were always ready to get on the job and get it done.

Back to the questions though. I glanced around the room as if I had heard the wrong thing, and then it was my turn to answer. I smirked and said, I guess I would have to say chocolate cake and as far as books are concerned, I'm not currently reading anything. His grin turned to somewhat of a frown. I didn't understand what I had said wrong. I thought we were supposed to share our answers for the two questions as I had just done. He then asked why I preferred chocolate cake over apple pie?

I gave my answer, which he agreed with, and most of the guys sitting around the table agreed as well. And then he asked, "Why aren't you reading any books?" And I told him, "Well, I've never really liked reading books and I don't have much time." He said, "Dude, we're all given the same amount of time in a day. A man that is not reading, is a man that is not learning and progressing. If you're not reading, then you are in the same place you were in years ago mentally. You are officially holding us back."

It was at that point that I understood what was happening in the room. He was providing an opportunity for us to share something personal about ourselves that most people would not know, thereby taking off some of the weight of the profession. Think about it for a minute, how many supervisors, that's you included, if it applies, don't know anything about the people they supervise or are responsible for? How many of them operate more like managers and taskmasters than they do individuals appreciating the value of those serving with them? Remember, it's the shield that matters, not just the spear. If your people know how much you care for them, they will care about what's important to you. But if they believe that you only look for ways to consolidate your self-interest, they will only do what's necessary and nothing else.

Getting back to my initial story. The next time I came back into his lineup, I had no idea what kind of dessert-oriented question I might get, but I'd dog-on sure had a book that I was reading, and for the right reasons. Once again, leadership is a two-way street. Many people in authority fail because they assume that their job is to simply direct others and that is all. But any great leader will tell you that the people they serve and are responsible for, have and will teach them just as much as they teach them as an authoritative figure.

So, I want you to think about that for just a moment. How do you lead? Are you maintaining the status quo and average expectation of your employees, classmates, coworkers, or even yourself? Or, do you come in every day ready to rock 'n' roll? Do you come in on fire and ready to work because you understand the purpose? When you understand the purpose of your position, and you understand the purpose of your job, the purpose of others shines through.

If you do not understand the purpose, then you will never fully commit. You will always second-guess everything that happens around you and to you in regards to your leadership role and the specific tasks that you are assigned to. Naturally, all the people that work under you and with you will struggle also. Remember, somebody is watching what you're doing, even when you don't know it. That's why you should always be operating at a level of excellence. Sergeant Rose had such an impact on his unit alone that other units around him began to take on the qualities and characteristics of his leadership style. That is what I'm talking about. Do you operate at a level that will cause other people to want to be better, to be excited about challenges coming their way, and be prepared to deal with whatever?

Can you lead in such a way that others will ignite the spark that burns down the acceptance of their excuses and internal complaints? Those are the things that continue to make you the victim, and them too. Scrap that garbage and burn it down. Burn down the house that stores your excuses, and be such an authentic and true leader that others feel uncomfortable lying and complaining around you. I'm talking about becoming such an effective leader that everybody knows you are driven by purpose, passion and progress.

I think back to the battle and the mighty 300, I can't help but admire how purpose led they were. Remember the quote I shared with you from the Spartan warrior Stelios. He said, "We are with you sire, for freedom, and Sparta, to the death!" What kind of a man does that? I'll tell you. It's a man that's been through the storms of life, and knows that the only way you're going to come out of the other side is to fight your way through. He offered this unsolicited statement without hesitation, and there was no way in the world you thought he was fluffing up the king's ego. Homeboy meant every word he said. Well, if that does not display a purpose driven leader, I don't know what would.

And let me reiterate something to you, he did not have much rank. That means that you don't have to be an elected official, and authoritative figure, or anyone with a special title to lead. So many people use their lack of permanent position as their excuse not to step up. Leadership really is a matter of influence, not power. The authority given should protect and build others up, it should not push them further down. Simply put, if people are following you because of the way you live and maneuver through business, school, or life, you are leading. How you're leading is the question!

5 Reasons That Leaders Must Understand Purpose:

- Purpose is the root of why any action takes place. Without it, people are operating with blind ambition.
- Purpose filled people are contagious, and demand a response to their dedicated lifestyle everywhere they go.
- Purpose is the starting block of any great journey. If you know your "Why," you can figure out "How."
- Purpose keeps you fueled when you want to quit.
- Purpose sets the tone for how you respond to challenges.

## *Free Game*

If you're going to lead anybody, you need to be disciplined. How are you going to tell anybody anything, and you can't even lead your own life? Now, if you're already in a leadership role, this doesn't mean you quit, you just knuckle up and make it happen! You are your first supervisor. I don't care what anybody else has to say in that matter. If you're going to lead, you better be able to dominate the small things first. If you say you're going to lose weight, then put down the cake. If you say you're going to be more patient, then stop running away from arguments. Small victories in the matter of self-discipline will take you a long way as a leader! I know it sounds repetitive, but it bears repeating. You are your first line of support.

## **What's On Your Chest?**

One of the greatest assets of a good and effective leader is the understanding of representation. Great leaders have what I've mentioned earlier, the 3-Musketeer mentality. They have one credo, and one alone. "All for one, and one for all." Reminds me of a time in high school when my track coach made me one of the team captains. My job was to make sure that the team got stretched out, and prepared for practices or track meets as they came about. He always said the same thing whenever we got on the bus to go to an away meet. "I want everybody to look down at your chest and tell me what you see on that uniform!" We would all answer simultaneously, "P!" P., stood for Page High School, that's right, home of the fierce Page Pirates! That was the school that we were going to represent.

Most high school students didn't fully understand the magnitude of representation. Just like the Olympics, or even war for that matter, when a small group of people represent a larger group of people, you are sending a message to those that you will encounter. You are telling them that you are the best of those from which you come. After we all gave Coach the response that he wanted, he would always look at us and say, "Now y'all better not embarrass me out there. Let's get right!"

For me, I didn't need Coach to get that point across. Culturally speaking, as an African-American man with family from the south, representation was always a huge thing. If anybody knew what your last name was, you better not act out of line or you would have 12 butt whoopings before you even got home. How times have changed, and not for the better in my opinion. For instance, I remember a time when I was hanging out with friends in my grandmother's neighborhood. The guys I was playing with weren't my usual crew, because it wasn't my neighborhood, but I knew them from school. They wanted to go past a certain street to play at a local park. While I wanted to go, and probably could have gotten away with it, I knew one thing for sure. Everybody in that neighborhood knew that I was Thelma and Grady Sutton's grandson.

That meant that I didn't have four eyes on me, I had the entire neighborhood's eyes on me. So, while they went on, after calling me chicken and a few other names, I was able to save the skin on my behind and make my way back down the street where I was supposed to have been in the first place. Even though it was on a small scale, that was a form of leadership. At an age when most kids cave to peer pressure, throw off restraint and excuse themselves from personal responsibility, I was functioning with family and consequences in mind. Understand, that representation still ties back to purpose. Purpose in this matter was me maintaining the integrity and character of my family name. Therefore, I was not willing to go down a simple street because it would leave a mark of disobedience and disregard for direction that could put a tarnish on how others viewed my amazing grandparents. Got it?

Let's just be real for a second, we all know that family in the neighborhood whose kids are just all over the place. I didn't call them the bad kids, you did, ha-ha. Don't act like I'm the only one that shakes their head when you just know they're about to get into something. Whenever you see them coming, everybody says "There goes the so-and-so kids. They're at it again." That's never a good thing unless the so-and-so kids are being a good representation of their family. How does that apply to leadership in your school, business, church, or even family? It's simple, everywhere you go, you should be the best representative you can be. That, is great leadership. In that sense, you were still putting up a shield against poor standards and lower expectations of those that you represent. You are still holding up the shield and utilizing the spear when necessary. The spear, in this case would be correcting the wrong assumptions made about you or those that you represent. If someone were to say that the team, business, or family that you come from sucks, it would be a utilization of your words and actions, the spear, to cut that false claim down.

But, no matter how talented or great you may be, if you lose sight of the purpose of either your role or the mission, you will throw off all restraints and care less about those that you represent. In leadership, this is unacceptable. That's because purpose and representation will always override personal desires. More times than not, you have not been forced into being a representative of a group. Therefore, it's up to you to make the most of what you have and be the best that you can be...on purpose!

## *Free Game*

Your purpose is not up for negotiation, stop using it as an excuse to be undisciplined in life. A lot of people have the audacity to believe they have no purpose, as if God made a mistake in creating them. I know, I know...not everybody believes in God, K.D. Right, but we can agree on the fact that everybody puts their shoes on one foot at a time, and breathes through their mouth and nose. That being the truth that it is, they are no greater than you. In most cases, they're just more resourceful and less of a crybaby. So, PURPOSE-UP...and get after it!

## **Started From The Bottom**

You may be wondering why I'm spending so much time on the concept of purpose in regards to leadership. If so, think of it like this. Imagine being given $500,000 to build your dream house on the perfect lot, in the perfect neighborhood, and in the perfect city. Just think about how excited you'd be to see the windows, walls and outside fixtures put in to place. Now, it's move in day and your whole family is so excited to see the inside of this perfect house. You walk up to the front door, past your perfect Kentucky green shaded grass lawn and pull out your key.

The anticipation is building as your husband and kids are standing huddled close behind you. As a mom, you can't wait to show them their new home. You open the door and step in, only to meet the smell of wet cement, and as you glance upward into your three-story dream house, you notice that you can see straight up to the third level roof. "What the heck is going on here" you'd yell. And as you almost break your cell phone punching in the contractor's phone number, your blood is boiling inside. "Hello! Where the heck is the freaking floor?" you'd shout. "Oh, that! Well, we wanted to save you as much money as we could, and get the house put up quickly so we laid some cheap slow dry cement and left the top floors open!" Naturally, this makes no freaking sense, at all! But hey...you saved a buck, right?

In the same way, purpose is the foundation on which the house of your life and decisions are built. If you shortcut the process of understanding purpose, you put the entire building in jeopardy. As a leader, it is your sole responsibility to know what grounds you're standing on and why. If the foundation is not set, the house will surely fall!

What's amazing though, is when you have examples of great leadership and groundwork around you. Allow me to share a true experience I had with a man that made his way to the top, but never ever forgot that he to, in the words of the philosophical professor Aubrey Graham, better known as "Drake" said, started from the bottom! I'm talking about my friend, and former Deputy Chief of Police, Dwight. Chief, as I called him, was known for treating people with respect, smiling, and just down right 'Gettin after it!"

I'll never forget that night. I had only been out of field training, and driving my own patrol car for about a year. I was definitely a 'Rookie Rookie', but I was determined to learn and grow while serving my community. One particular shift, while working from 8pm-7am, I pulled over a car for having an expired license plate. As I approached the vehicle driver side window, I noticed there were two people in the car. Mind you, it was around 2am and directly in front of one of the local rough neighborhoods. There's no diss there, but night time in that area had proven to be full of "excitement" some might say. Not the best place in the world to be rolling solo, but the job was the job.

I introduced myself to the driver, and got all the information I needed before returning to verify things on my police computer. As my patrol car lights shined like Christmas tree bulbs through the dark skies, I noticed a second set of lights flashing from behind and closing distance quickly. I was thrown off because I didn't call for an assist car, and the lights weren't on the top of the vehicle, they were in the windshield. This could mean only one thing, a high-ranking supervisor.

Now, I was more nervous than I was dealing with the neighborhood I was in on this traffic stop. Why was a ranking officer pulling up behind me? Did I do something wrong? Was I about to get fired and have to walk home in my draws and tube socks? You know how it is when supervisors come around unexpectedly, you freak the heck out and ask yourself dumb questions. I could see the silhouette of a person as the unknown officer exited their vehicle. They crossed between the front of their car and the rear of mine. As is police custom, when a fellow officer approaches from the rear, you roll the window down so that you can still see what's in front of you while listening to your assist.

As I rolled the passenger side window down, I looked up, only to see the chest of an officer wearing long sleeves and a tie, coming into view. Talk about a slow-motion uncomfortable feeling. Then I realized it was Chief Dwight! At the time, I didn't know him that well, but every time I had seen him, I just got that positive vibe if that makes sense. He was just always the type of boss you hoped to work for. "Hey there young man, what do you have here on this fine early morning?" he asked with a huge smile on his face. Chief never turned his head towards me while talking. That wasn't a sign of disrespect, it was the tactics of a seasoned officer. He didn't know what I was dealing with at the time, and because he was standing next to my vehicle, he was more exposed to danger than I was.

"Oh, not much sir, just an expired registration" I responded. "Outstanding, is everything Signal 50?" he asked. Signal 50 was one of the 10 Codes that we used to communicate certain things amongst one another. The most notorious and commonly used code between both first responders and military would be the phrase "Ten Four or 10-4", meaning 'Correct, Affirmative or Yes." I continued to verify the driver's information, and though he had some prior incidents, nothing jumped out at me. "Yes sir, I'm Signal 50 chief. Thanks for checking on me, I'm good from here sir. No need to hang out here if you're headed home," I told him. "Well, I was just finishing up a supervising shift when I saw your lights in the distance, and figured I'd stop and give ya a hand. What do you say we get these gentlemen on their way and make it a great morning for us all?" he stated. "Sure thing sir, I'm just finishing up this warning ticket, and we'll be good to go." I said. I exited my vehicle and approached on the driver side while Chief moved up from the rear passenger side. I gave the driver all that he needed, and the warning ticket, that he was supremely grateful for, and then I wished him well on his way. As the vehicle pulled off, I shook the Chief's hand and thanked him for stopping to check on me. You see, most Lieutenants, Captains, Deputy Chief's and Chiefs don't wear full duty gear like patrol officers do. Because they operate in more of an administrative role. They typically wore a slick duty belt, shiny shoes, their firearm, one magazine, a walkie talkie and a single pair of handcuffs.

Needless to say, it was cool seeing Chief still getting after it in his shiny shoes. We often talked about how the shiny shoes meant you weren't a real cop anymore. It meant that you were a desk jockey. Not chief, every encounter I had with him from that day forward was nothing short of a good time. I'm not calling any names out, but it's EXTREMELY rare to see anyone above a Sergeant, out in the field and helping patrol. Chief Dwight was known for being, as we say in street lingo, "That Dude!" Not only did Chief never allow his rank to get to his head, but he never lost sight of the purpose of his position. He wasn't above any of us, even when he was above all of us. He operated from a position of positive influence. He knew that without influence, leaders were non-existent. Lastly, he valued good results over good recognition. That is the sign of a true leader. One that never loses his or her hold on the purpose of their role, and mission!

## The Purpose Is To Learn By Learning

You see, in the police academy we had to learn how to defend ourselves and other people in case we were ever confronted with violence. The particular training that we underwent was called SCAT, Subject Control and Arrest Techniques. It was basically the police equivalent of hand to hand combat. Naturally, the police academy is a mixed bunch of both male and female recruits. Being that I grew up in the military and trained in martial arts most of my life, I thoroughly enjoyed that aspect of the training. Not everyone thought the same way though. This was especially true for some of the ladies in my academy class. I remember sparring and training with a particular female. I didn't want to kick with full extension, strike with full force, or apply maximum pressure if I got her into a chokehold.

I couldn't break past what my mother used to tell me as a child. "Son, always do your best never to hit a woman," she said. Though I knew that it was necessary to do it, I did my best not to force maximum impact on to this particular classmate of mine because I didn't believe she could take it. My instructors were watching me, because they knew I was excelling in the class at a rapid pace. And then I heard one of them scream my name. I was startled to be honest with you, and caught off guard because

I didn't know what I had done wrong. "Wilson," he yelled. "Yes sir," I said. "What the heck do you think you're doing? Why are you holding back," He asked? "Well sir, I didn't want to hurt her," I responded. He started fuming, "Do you think the person on the street is going to take it easy on her? You think they give a crap that she's a female, or do you think they're going to do whatever they have to do in order to escape?" I knew exactly what he meant in that moment. "No sir, they won't take it easy on her," I replied. "Well then, you know what to do don't you," He asked?

After that conversation, I didn't hold back and began to swing with full force, kicked with full extension, and applied pressure at my maximum ability for training purposes. Afterwards, he pulled me to the side and said, "I know you're trying to be a good leader, but you are being a bad leader and poor training partner when you allow her to think that she is withstanding something that she really can't handle at the moment. It's not up to you to decide whether or not this profession is for her. If you don't do your job, as a squad leader, and future officer, you are failing. The purpose is to learn, not to patty cake."

Again, it all made perfect sense to me. I was trying to spare her the pain of the fight, because I thought that's what a good leader would do. But, I didn't realize that I was actually hurting her, and putting her life in danger by doing what I was doing. If you're still struggling to understand what I mean, think of it like this. If any of you have kids, or young siblings that can't swim, a common thing to use for them are floaties. You know, those blow up bubble bands that go over their arms, around their waist or around their legs? When kids jump in the water and can't swim properly, those floating devices actually do more damage than good.

It makes them believe they can float, and swim when they really can't. If you take those floats off, and throw that same child into the deep end, they'll panic, and drown. As a parent or family member, that's a terrible thing to do, and is not leadership at all. Instead, taking the time to teach them, or put them through swim classes would be better. It's not different in the academy. I was actually doing her wrong by letting her think she was taking shots, and applying techniques correctly. Leadership is being a great training partner, mentally, physically, spiritually and emotionally. The purpose is to learn.

**Shield Over Spear Chapter Summary**

In this chapter we've tackled the foundation of the leader...purpose. This ties directly into the philosophy of Shield Over Spear for obvious reasons. If a leader attacks challenges and issues without an understanding of the mission or purpose, chaos ensues. Imagine seeing a general charging on to the battlefield as enemy fighters approach. Now imagine soldiers calling for him to stop, as he refuses to heed their call. All he knows is, there is a fight on the horizon. Then, all of the soldiers take cover as bombs drop from the sky onto the battlefield. The general doesn't make it, and is lost because he ran aimlessly into battle without knowing the purpose of the soldier's patience. If he had known they were waiting for an airstrike, he would have lived. But, he ran headlong into a fight while criticizing those waiting behind the trees. He never asked the question, "Why?"

On the other hand, by taking the time to ask the question, "What am I doing and why am I doing it?" a leader is able to push harder and further than they ever thought possible. When you have a purpose behind what you do, what can stop you, if what you're doing is for the right reason? Purpose will always demand the leader to sacrifice their pride, ego, and selfishness. That is something you do not need to carry back on your shield, let it die and stay where it is. Purpose allows you to answer the question, is my presence more of a hinderance, or benefit to those I serve? From here, we move into the next staple in any great leader's war bag...Vision! Now that the foundation is set, it's time to aim at the target!

# Principle 2: Vision

*The most pathetic person in the world is some one who has sight but no vision!*

*-Helen Keller*

**Vision,** defines the ideal future state, the mental picture, or the dream!

King Leonidas was a problem for the politicians. He wasn't liked by the political counsel in the movie, but he was loved by his people. The politicians only thought about ways for them to keep what they had and appear to care, without having the heart to follow it up. The brave king was disliked because he could see the bigger picture. The local politicians dreamt of power and safety, while the king realized that power, and safety were only maintained when freedom was present. Independence was dependent on those willing to go the distance for others.

They wanted to negotiate with the tyrant Xerxes, and see how much of their land they could keep if they surrendered, but not the king. He knew that negotiation meant slavery for all. He had prepared all of his life for a battle of this magnitude. He had dreamed of it, he visualized it, and it was something he had trained for as a young man. He knew that one day the biggest battle of his life would arrive, and then, there it was at his doorstep. The very first thing he did was take inventory of resources and locations. Once he had it mapped out in his head, it was just a matter of execution. But it wasn't enough for the king to see it in his own mind, he had to explain it to his men.

What good would it be for the great king to see a victory that includes his men, without including his men? That is the next strong point of any leader, the ability to see it and create a picture for others to follow after. What areas are you negotiating in when it comes to your vision? When you look at the possibilities, in what space are you giving yourself an emergency exit in? What area of your life and leadership development are you taking a knee and surrendering to others or your emotions?

The king was an unreasonable man, and rightfully so. The word, unreasonable, means to be irrational, against the norm, contrary, and excessive. When looking at an army that wants to decimate your entire country, was there really any other way to be, than unreasonable? For the king to be reasonable, he would have looked at the possibilities from the perspective of a defeated man, not a warrior king. Again, what do you see, and what's holding you back? What fear provoking sight, or idea is hindering you from casting your eyes on the vastness of the world, and seeing what 'could be?'

**Questioning Vision**

There are a few things that vision creates. Things that will prove beneficial in the long run, but first, there are questions that must be answered.

- Vision sets the roadmap for what you're pursuing.
    - What thought, feeling, or person has the power to derail you from staying on course?

_____

_____

- Vision defines the optimal desired future state, and the mental picture.
    - How close is your present picture to your future picture?

_____

- Vision allows for specific features to be seen.

    o What is the vision you have of yourself at your best? What does it look like, smell like, taste like, feel like?

___

- Vision builds culture.

    o What type of environment do you create as a leader? Based on what you see, how will people feel, and be treated? Will they be appreciated, valued, easily replaced, ignored, etc. around you?

___

## More Than Meets The Eye

Vision is not confined to the natural eye alone. If truth be told, you can see more with your eyes closed than you can with your physical eyes open. Let's talk physiology for a minute. Did you know that before you have that great 'Aha' moment, most of the visual portion of your brain shuts down? Why though? If almost 80% of our information is taken in through sight, why in the world would the brain want to shut off the visual part of the mind? It actually makes a lot of sense when explained. Allow me to do that for you. Ask yourself this question, have you ever stared at a computer screen or your cell phone and just found yourself in a blank daze? Ever been working on the internet and had to look away, walk outside, or turn the computer off to actually think about what you were supposed to be thinking about in the first place? As for the first statement about the shutdown, it's because there's too much information coming in at one time for your mind to focus on one centralized point.

Ever noticed that whenever somebody asks you a question about duration of time, something that happened in the past or the like, you glance up into the sky to the right? Some of you are doing it right now as a matter of fact. You're doing that to clear the images in your head and focus on the question at hand. That's part of the power of vision. It's great to multi-task, but in doing so you realize that you're not putting all of your effort in to one target. That's why I say that vision is not limited to your physical eye sight alone. It's more a matter of your internal eye sight than your outer eye sight that leaders must truly harness.

That's why Stevie Wonder and Ray Charles were leaders in the music industry. They've seen more with their internal eyes than most people see with natural eyes wide open. Though they lacked the ability to see with their physical eyes, their internal visualization skills were through the roof. Think about how much focus it took to learn to see through feeling and hearing. When placing your hands-on keys, and being able to teach others how to do the same...all without your natural eyesight. There has to be something greater.

They could see with their hands better than most could see through their eyes. They could see the crowds in their minds, but even more, they could see the keys on the pianos they dominated every time they sat down. It was the sound that allowed them to see. What do you see when you close your eyes? What image pops up that won't let you live a boring and settled life? By settled, I don't mean family and such things. No, you know what I mean. When you've lost your bite, your hunger, and appetite to grow. What's your mission in life? What do you see?

If your answer is, nothing, that's a huge problem, and probably why you're in the same place you've been in for the longest. You can't see anything, so you won't do anything, naturally. I'm challenging you to open your eyes, dream again, and see again. When you do that, as a leader, the people under you have something to fight for. Sometimes those in the back can't see the purpose in the front, but if a leader can understand the purpose and provide his or her team with a clear picture of the 'what', the purpose and vision will fall into place on its own.

## *Free Game*

If you can't see the problem, you are probably part of the problem. What does that even mean, right? More times than not, we're shadowboxing. That means, we're swinging at the future, hoping to land the perfect punch with no idea of what we're swinging at, or if it's even going to make a difference if we do. Step back from your emotions, locate the root of the issue, and attack it with precise shots.

### **Adjusted Sights**

I remember working the night shift as an officer. As the sun went down and the darkness took over, I began to notice that my eyes adjusted to the lack of light. Even when walking into the back of someone's yard on a call, or in an alley. Somehow, I could still see. My eyes had adjusted in order to detect movement in the darkness. Likewise, leaders have built in night vision goggles. They can see in the darkest of times because they've been through enough to know how to readjust in the midst of chaos. They understand the purpose, and therefore their ability to see when things don't make sense to the natural eye, takes over.

As a graduate of North Carolina Agricultural and Technical State University, or better known as A&T, such a time was birthed from four of my fellow Aggies. On February 1, 1960, just three years after my mother was born, four young black male students sat down at an 'all white' lunch counter at the Woolworth Store in Greensboro, NC. Due to the racial injustice of the 'separate but not equal' clause of the law, these students decided they had endured enough. So, to combat racial injustice, they had a 'vision.' That vision became reality when they marched into the store and sat down. As members of the black community, when David Richmond, Franklin McCain, Ezell Blair Jr. and Joseph McNeil sat down...people of color across the nation stood up! Some of you may be wondering why I'm sharing such a story.

Well, besides bragging about my brothers, you need to see the bigger picture. From the time the first black body stepped foot on American soil, and in many ways, even till today, there has been a cloud in the sky. A gray cloud that reminds us of dark times when black and brown bodies were kidnapped, tortured, mercilessly assaulted and forced into slavery. If that isn't a representation of darkness, and night, I don't know what is. And yet, in 1960 when people of color were still very much seen as inferior, and as 'other,' these four young men turned on their night vision goggles and made some noise in the middle of a dim time. They lit a fire under the seats of people nationwide because they could see something greater than what they were being offered.

If your vision doesn't set someone else free in an area of their life, you're missing it. If what you see doesn't build someone up to make them better, then you have narcissistic eyes. Great leaders are able to see in the darkest of times because they're fueled by something bigger than themselves. As a leader, it's up to you to make sure you're not too comfortable in the light.

**Bigger Than Blocking**

In the movie 300, there is a particular scene after the first battle where the men have broken rank and go on a solo destructive rampage. Left and right, the Persian army continues to fall. The king, after cutting people down with his sword continued to move forward, never retreating. As he dances through the opposing soldiers with sword in hand, from a distance outside of the screen, an enemy approached. For those of you that love movies like I do, you may have found yourself yelling at the television telling the king to watch out. Again though, the king could see just fine. After shuffling his feet, and turning toward the enemy soldier, he offers him one piece of his equipment, the shield. And he hit him with it. I mean, knocked him on his butt, and then ran him through with his sword.

All of us in the crowd went nuts! The shield speaks for itself. It is very much a weapon. The "BOOM" of the collision is enchanting. The shield stops attack, safeguards from weather, covers for concealment, crushes things under pressure, and stops things from moving forward. All of these things, leaders do. Great leaders stop attacks on their team, they see ahead and address problematic situations that reign down frustration, they conceal them from unnecessary exposure, they crush excuses and stop them from moving forward without clear sight. It's what good leaders do!

## *Free Game*

My pastor once said something to me that was profound, and yet extremely helpful. He said in regards to your belief, particularly in the realms of faith, "Hold loosely to the picture, and tightly to the promise." That means, sometimes the very things that we are willing to believe with all of our strength, could be coming through in a different way and not holding the image or the wrapping paper, if you will, that we imagined. Don't get so overwhelmed with the picture that you forget the significance of its beauty, purpose and reward.

### **Hey Kid! You're Up!**

While working downtown one night, still a rookie fresh out of the police academy, I found myself standing in front of a packed club. It was the custom for night shift officers to make their way downtown if they weren't stuck on a call, so that they could help out the bike units with what we called the 'Club Dump.' In the city I served, there were 4-6 well known night clubs and bars within a 2-3 street radius. This particular club was always good for having a few people that stocked up on what we call 'liquid courage' aka alcohol. You've probably seen it on a movie, or maybe even in person. Somebody drinks a beer or two and now they think they're the incredible Hulk.

Well, that was the norm from Thursday through Sunday night downtown. At the time, I had been able to solve all of my issues using words and persuasion, as I was trained to do. I hadn't encountered anyone that refused to help me, or help themselves.

I also hadn't engaged any drunk people ready to fight at that particular time either.

I dropped by one of the clubs as aforementioned to check on the bike officers. "Stick around, it's a packed house and there's bound to be some hot heads unfortunately" one said. Now, the Sergeant at the time was known for being a bad mofo! Not in a negative way, you just knew that if you went too far, he'd meet you in the middle of the road if you know what I mean. It was almost time for the club to let out when the bouncers started chucking belligerent partiers out the front door. Most of them would be on their way and catch a cab or walk. Occasionally, a few needed some words of encouragement. This particular night, I stood in the back of the pack. As a new officer, I felt protected because I could not see myself dealing with a strong, drunk, and angry person bent on having their way just yet. I could on the other hand, see myself helping the team if things got out of hand a bit.

"Hey new kid!" the Sergeant said. "Yes sir!" I replied. "Come on up front, the next one that gets thrown out is yours" he said, as the rest of his squad laughed. I was petrified, I just couldn't see myself dealing with this yet. I mean, what if the guy wants to fight or won't listen to me? What if he snuck a gun in there and tries to shoot me in the face? Why the heck did I come down here?" I asked myself as I walked to the front of the group. All of a sudden, I realized something. I signed up for this, and if I was going to be a well-rounded officer, I would need to be able to deal with different types of people. Drunk ones included. While the butterflies were attempting to bust out of my stomach, my mind began to settle down as I expanded my vision to meet my reality. I was ready!

Thankfully, that night went smooth and nobody got out of

hand. I was grateful to the sergeant though, because he put me in a place where I had no choice but to see myself winning, no matter the situation. In leadership, you do no good to your team if you shelter them from things they don't want to see or engage.

Now, I'm not saying that you should throw them into situations they truly aren't prepared for, but just like a parent that never assigns chores to the children in a home, you end up doing more bad than good. So, that doesn't mean you force challenges their way, but it also doesn't mean you let them close their eyes to life either. Adversity often forces us to expand our vision, because in that moment, all we want to see is a way out. For the leader, when adversity arises, they look around to see what the next move is going to be in order to win. Why? Challenging times tell you the truth about yourself, knuckle up! Win or Win BIG!

## **Believing Is Seeing**

In 2015, legendary NBA super star, Steph Curry of the Golden State Warriors, made a ridiculous 3-Point shot to tie the game against the Pelicans. This may not seem like much, but I didn't mention that he made the shot with 6ft 10in Anthony Davis charging directly at him. Yes, the human tree, A. Davis. To add insult to injury...he made the shot with his eyes closed! That's right, Steph Curry dropped a 3-Pointer on an almost 7ft defender with his eyes wide shut. Now, many people say that he released the ball before he closed his eyes, and that he was merely bracing for impact. That's understandable. But, this is Steph Curry we're talking about here. According to ESPN, Steph Curry made 77 consecutive 3-Pointers and hit 94 of his attempted 100 shots from outside of the paint over a span of time. Come on y'all, 77 triples in a row! Let's just say that it doesn't matter what anybody says here, I'm saying he did it with his eyes closed.

No matter the argument, there is one thing that will go uncontested. Steph Curry sees every shot before he shoots it. As a leader, he carries both purpose and vision for, and with his team. He knows that if he's going to be of any use to the team, his internal and external eyes have to be intact. This comes with repetition, practice and unprecedented focus.

What about you though? Can your team rely on you to hit the winning shot? Can they rely on you to see what needs to be done and move on it? Or, do they have to see it for you? Do they have to spoon feed your next move because it's easier for you to close your eyes and let them do the hard work? If you're going to lead, you better get used to leading with your eyes open, so that one day you can make the winning shot with your eyes wide shut!

**<u>3 Keys To Expanding Your Vision</u>**

1. Update Your Prescription
2. Study
3. Put Something On The Line

There are a few things you can do to expand your vision if you feel like you're just moving forward aimlessly. One of the first things you should do is UPDATE YOUR PRESCRIPTION. What that means is, just like when you've had a pair of glasses for so long, the clarity begins to fade. The old prescription simply cannot keep up with the new things that your eyes have to encounter every day. I would charge you to look at a time when you could see clearer than ever, and compare that time to now. What has changed? Is it your environment, or is it you?

Another good suggestion would be to make sure you revisit the people you're surrounding yourself with. If the people around you are taking more out of you than they deposit, or at least maintaining an equal balance...make the necessary adjustments.

The second thing I want you to do is STUDY! Man, so many people disregard the need to continuously learn. Whenever you get to a place in life when you feel like you've got it down, it's time to move. If you're ever the smartest person in the room consistently, it's time to expand your circle or change rooms. The best part about vision is that it can evolve with the things that it's introduced to. Ask yourself the question, what don't I know about my industry? Why haven't I taken the time to deal with these things that I know aren't my strong suits? And, most of all...what am I going to do about it?

The last thing you can do is PUT SOMETHING ON THE LINE. In this day and age, we typically have vision for ourselves, never others. Give yourself healthy consequences. Question! If you had to become the #1 person in your class, field, profession, etc. in one month, or else your family would be forced into homelessness, what would you do? I know the answer. You'd become the #1 person, right? So, apply that same pressure to your life right now without the dark results of failure looming over you. I'm asking you to put something valuable on the line when you consider what you're looking for in life, and what you're looking at in the future. I've learned that when you attach other people to your success, the odds of you giving up are slim to none.

My question to you is, what do you see? Do the eyes of your heart still work? You know what I mean? When you were a kid, there was nothing off limits to your mind. What happened? Can you go back to the moment when you stopped seeing opportunities, and started focusing on obstacles? I know many of you will say, "K.D., it's called life. It's called, being an adult." While I understand the excuse, I don't accept it. Do you know why? Because Albert Einstein said, "Imagination is more important than knowledge. Knowledge is limited, imagination encircles the world." What he was trying to get across to his listeners was this, keep the eyes of your heart open if you want to do something significant in the world.

**The Sight Factor**

Vision determines your victory. Not only does it determine whether or not you succeed or fail, but it determines the process from start to finish. There are simply some things that you are not permitted to do when you're after certain things in life. Vision lets you know what kind of friends you can have and places that you can or cannot hang out at. Vision determines what time you go to sleep and what time you wake up. It determines the types of food you eat and how you treat your body and your mind. Vision determines the victory in all aspects.

Why would I say such a thing? It's quite simple really. A doctor would not spend time with a basketball player if she was trying to become a heart surgeon. An eagle would not spend time with a shark if it was trying to learn how to fly. Vision determines associations. If you want to be successful in anything, particularly as a leader, you need to surround yourself with people and be in places that are conducive to the mission. That is where standards come from. If a leader does not set a standard for his or her team, they leave them to their own devices. Where there is no standard, recklessness runs free. One of the greatest gifts you can give your team or the people that you are leading is a clear understanding of the vision. That of course, comes after the purpose, but nonetheless, the vision is critical to success. If you can help your team see what you see, then they will be willing to do what you do.

Remember, determination is onset by way of clear direction. Visionless leaders and teams constantly run themselves into the ground because they are always scrambling to react to a problem instead of having the wherewithal and understanding of how to respond. If someone throws a ball at my head unexpectedly, I will naturally react and hopefully catch it or duck out of the way. But, if I am at a baseball field watching a practice just to the right of first base, because of my environment and ability to see what is happening, I am able to respond with a glove and hand or a movement laid out in my mind instead of reacting. That's what vision does; it allows you to remain in control because you were able to see things that others could not see. You can respond to things, while others can only react and hope for the best.

Here's a question for you. In terms of your leadership ability, how well are you able to see? On a scale of 1 to 10, with 1 being the least, and 10 being the greatest. How would you rate your ability to look beyond your own feet and issues to see what needs to be accomplished?

_____

_____

Question! How do you see yourself? Repeat this with me. "The me I see, is the me I'll be." That means exactly what it sounds like. The way you see yourself is the way you will respond at all times. So, you have to have a solid vision for the person that you want to become while steadily building the person that you are. The greatest leaders are the ones that understand what's going on within themselves first. Think about a time you were under someone else's leadership, and that person was one of your favorite authoritative figures.

Below, write down the characteristics and things that made them stand out and made you appreciate the way they operated. Now, how does that compare to the qualities and characteristics that you hold and apply as a leader yourself? I'm just trying to get you to think outside of yourself and look at how those things can be duplicated and bring about success.

---

---

---

## Shield Over Spear Chapter Summary

It goes without saying that when freedom is on the line, anything goes. But, what about for your team? What about you? If you cannot see, then you cannot effectively shield them or yourself from things you should not be dealing with. By facing your issues, and meeting your team where they are, you will begin to see tangible change. When you tell your team that you see a victory, they should feel safe behind the shielded picture you've painted. Again, when they can see what you see...they believe. Every single thing that we do in life is based on one word, and one word alone...belief. You will act on what you believe, at all times, and in every single way. From picking out your shoes, to going to work, to cooking food, or playing with your kids...belief is attached. So, what will your team believe based on what you see? Most of all, what will you believe that will change the dynamics of your life? Now that you've locked in purpose, and vision...let's test your metal!

# Principle 3: Commitment

*There are only two options when it comes to commitment; you're either in or you're out!*

*-Pat Riley*

**Commitment**, means to pledge yourself to, bind, be obligated, and give in trust.

There's a section in the film when the Spartan army is marching towards the battlefield. Soon after, they come to an intersection, and encounter other Greeks. The king welcomes them, and invites them to join in the ranks. The other leader scoffs and tells the king that a rumor was spreading that Sparta had committed large numbers to fight off the Persian war lord. The Greek leader is disappointed because he only sees the king, and his 300. The king then launches a brutal counter attack with words. He points to three men in the Greek leader's group, and asked a simple question, "What is your profession?"

The three responses were...Sculptor, Blacksmith, and Potter. The mighty king then turns his head, barely losing eye contact with the Greek leader, as he yells back to his men, "SPARTANS...what is your profession?" To which the response is a roaring, "AROO...AROO...AROO!" as shields clanked and spears jolted into the air with clinched fists around them. The Greek leader understood now. He understood that the king had brought men that had committed their entire lives to the art of combat, while he had brought men with no experience at all. The king said, "See old friend. I brought more soldiers than you did!" The key word there is commitment.

As a leader, what, and who, are you bringing to the intersection? Are you bringing uncommon commitment that will break through the barriers of complacency and forfeiture that plagues society today? Or, will you show up with great expectation, but no intention of actually engaging the challenges set before you? The beautiful part is that you can still choose to be either. You can be a Spartan warrior, or a Greek volunteer. One person was willing to fight for what they believed in, while the other was only willing when the odds looked to be in their favor. Those that are committed, make their own odds. The dice they roll, always lands on the desired number. There is no luck for people like that. There is only discipline, action, and freedom.

You will never ever commit to that which you do not believe in. It simply will not happen, it just won't. If you don't believe in something then you have no foundation on which to stand. If you have no foundation, then you have no purpose, and if you have no purpose, there is no point. Commitment has less to do with the rest of the world and more to do with you keeping the promise you made to yourself. When you get to a place where you are consistently committed, what can stop you?

Commitment has to come from the inside, and hold things in place. It cannot come from other people pushing and prodding you to do something. If it does, what will you do when they're not around? True leaders commit when nobody is looking, so that they can move and respond when everyone is. The Bible even talks about commitment. Jesus once said that you will know the shepherd from the hireling by their level of commitment. The shepherd will put down a staff and pick up its rod to defend the sheep against the wolves. A hireling will drop everything, and sacrifice the sheep in order to save itself. Commitment, again comes from position, and position is birthed out of purpose and clear sight.

One reason that people often fall short as leaders, and even in matters of personal discipline, is lack of commitment. But, every time I see a commitment issue, I can always link it back to the first two principles of purpose and vision. Occasionally you will find the one that does have a purpose and vision but simply operates in fear. Some people say that fear is helpful when it comes to remaining committed. Like anger, I believe that fear will only last but for so long.

Being an emotion or state of mind, fear will not remain at all times and therefore will open up a window where the person has to make a decision on what they're going to do next. For instance, some people work terribly hard at their job for fear of losing their position. If they lose their position, then they lose their salary. If they lose their salary, they may lose their house. Well that equation makes perfect sense to me, but it is no way to live or function. If your commitment level is solely based on reward, what will happen when the reward is taken away?

To all of you reading this book that are directly in charge of hiring and firing others, listen carefully please. Your people will commit, and achieve the necessary goals when you provide them a safe environment that does not manipulate their productivity by way of fear. In the Pixar movie, Monsters Inc., the monsters would use portal doors to sneak into children's bedrooms and scare them. The screams of scared children produced energy and power for the monsters to use in their world. This was the norm until one day, two monsters went off the grid and developed a relationship with one of the children that laughed at them instead of screaming. In the end, the monsters realized that laughter actually created two to three times the amount of energy and power than screaming did. So, the focus of the company shifted from monsters terrifying kids, to monsters becoming hilariously funny. It was a win for both sides.

You are that monster! If you are walking around attempting to scare your team, members, employees, or even yourself into creating energy, you are doing it all wrong. When a person laughs with you, more times than not, they feel safe with you. If they feel safe with you, but also understand that their level of commitment factors in to the success of the overall team...they will fight to win for you. But, if you treat them like slaves, they will act like them. You heard me, and that goes for you too. If you treat yourself like a nobody, you'll act like it. They too will do only what's required, and as soon as they see your level of authority dwindling, they will attack you. In my opinion, rightfully so. Nobody likes a task master, but we sure do love a balanced person that leads the charge by becoming a champion for themselves and their people first.

## *Free Game*

Les Brown said, "You are committed to mediocrity or greatness, choose one!" How true is this statement? We cannot live with a double mind. Either we're going to go after it, or we're not. Stop playing games and make a decision already.

### **Leaders Need To Be**

This doesn't really require a lot of explaining so I'll just cut to the chase and let you know what you need to be. Effective leaders must be:

- **M**otivated
- **E**mpathetic
- **M**ature
- **O**ptimistic
- **R**esilient
- **A**ble
- **B**old
- **L**oyal
- **E**ducated

I remember just about every great leader that I ever had, even from my childhood days. That's because great leaders are **"MEMORABLE!"** If nobody remembers what you did...you didn't do anything!

## The Embodiment Of Shield Over Spear

There is a story, a true story at that, about a soldier that fought in World War II with no weapon in hand. His name was Corporal Desmond Doss. He felt that his purpose was to save lives in the middle of the war, and the best way he could serve his country was in doing so, but without taking a life himself. Because of his deep-rooted belief that God had created him for such a time as that, he enlisted in the Army. In the movie, 'Hacksaw Ridge', it illustrates what happened to the brave soldier. He was ridiculed, cast off, and beaten by his fellow Americans. That's right, it wasn't foreigners that attacked him first, it was the men enlisted right next to him. Side Note...keep that in mind when you're selecting your friends. But why? Easy! They could not see what he could see, and they did not believe what he believed. Because of their inability to see his purpose and vision, they questioned his commitment. In the end, his commitment level would save 75 American souls, and those of the opposition as well.

For the sake of clarity, Desmond Doss joined the army, and notified the ranking officials that he refused to pick up a weapon, but still wanted to serve. He was what most consider, a conscientious objector. This is a person that for reasons of the conscience, refuse to comply with specific requirements, particularly in the military. From my understanding, because he was going to be a combat medic, there was no rule in the military mandating that he must carry a firearm, nor train with one. Once again, he was treated terribly by his own, and this was from the lowest ranking enlisted soldier all the way to the top of the military ranks. They even tried to have him court martialed, which means, to try in military court with military specific charges. But, he did not quit, and he stayed committed because he had a vision and a purpose to fulfill. In the movie, which again is based on a true story, they go to war against the Japanese in World War II.

Upon their arrival, they end up on a treacherous cliff that was eventually named Hacksaw Ridge. This ridge was basically a 400-foot vertical cliff of which was scaled by using cargo type nets and rope ladders. As the American troops suffered mass casualties and terrible loss of life atop that cliff side, there was barely anywhere to retreat to. Like our modern day first responders, when everyone was running away, he ran in. Corporal Doss disobeyed a direct order to retreat, and stayed committed to what he believed God had created him to do...save lives. And wouldn't you know it, the very people that gave him the hardest times were the ones that he pulled to safety.

What he did, went far beyond that of a hero. According to the story, while facing death, being injured, and trying to balance the mental ramifications of the environment, he single-handedly saved 75 lives by lowering them off the side of the cliff. He was fueled by purpose, driven by vision, and sold on commitment. It has been confirmed from my understanding that on top of that ridge, as he faced unspeakable and relentless odds, he prayed a prayer to God.

"Dear God, please help me get just one more", he said. He prayed that prayer over 50 times, and between the two of them, he and God worked out a deal. Corporal Doss held up and maintained a level of commitment that most would never fathom. Even our most hardened warriors, that being the Navy

SEALs, Recon and Green Berets would never voluntarily go into a war zone without a weapon I'm sure. But as previously stated, one will never commit to that which one does not believe in. He believed and therefore he did. He did, so that others could live. Stay the course, and stay committed!

How committed are you to the process of BECOMING an amazing leader? On a scale of 1-10, with 1 being the lowest and 10 being the highest level...how committed are you?

---

One of the greatest misconceptions about leadership is that it has to come with a label, as if the label gives a person super powers. Desmond Doss was a leader because he was committed to saving lives without taking them. He endured the process that anchored his truth into the hearts and minds of those opposing him, his fellow soldiers. His truth was this, "I will...not quit!"

So, when the time had come to be the valiant soldier that everyone claimed they were destined to be, Doss was the only one that stepped in to deliver on the promise that he made to himself. Did you catch that? The promise he made to himself! It's not the title that makes the leader, it's the attitude of the leader that earns him/her the title. Promotion doesn't mean promise of success. There are plenty of suck ups in life that have smooched their way into a role they aren't qualified to handle. Make sure that you're not one of those people! If so, cut that mess out. Oh sure, they wanted the prize, but they were terrified of the process.

When it comes to commitment, describe a time when you stuck it out even when you wanted to quit. What made you stay, and what did you learn about yourself in the process?

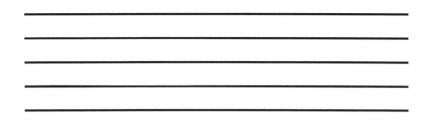

## *Free Game*

If you only remain consistent when it's convenient, you'll fail when it's not! Consistency is the arch nemesis of complacency and convenience. You should actually look for ways to make things a tad harder for yourself whenever you feel like you're starting to slow down. In my opinion, it's better to add some calculated stress to your life now, and acclimate your mind to overcoming that before life tosses something at you while you're chilling on the couch and totally unprepared. Plan to win, or plan to fail, and shut up about it.

### **Cutting Dead Weight**

Every year, people make the journey to a distant land in search of glory. That level of achievement they seek, comes by way of "The Climb." I'm talking about Mt. Everest, the highest peak on earth. When climbing Mt. Everest, you have to acknowledge something that most people wouldn't dare consent to. You have to agree that once you reach a certain point, if you don't come down on your own, you're not coming down at all. You have to commit! You have to commit, unto death, if need be. Mt. Everest is just shy of 30,000 ft. That's right at the level that a commercial jet ascends to. To date, the journey to the summit has claimed roughly 293 lives, that's including climbers and their guides. One could assume that it's for that reason alone that only about 4,800 have summited the monstrous mountain. To the natural eye that seems like a lot, but it's not when you think about the first recorded summit that took place in 1953. Even more so the fact that there are 7.71 billion people in the world today. Yeah soak that in for a minute. It's easy to look at a big number and feel small, but these people made themselves big.

This takes us into an amazing example of why purpose, and vision are so necessary before commitment. Like this mountain ascension, you have to be able count the cost of your journey. As a leader and individual, are the things you're pursuing worth all that you're investing? Why have an unfulfilled vision of climbing the mountain without purpose and calculation? Why have a purpose, but create no vision or step into commitment? It takes everything you have to summit Everest. One way or another, it's going to take everything you have to be the type of leader that you honestly can be, and the type that your team deserves. The air gets thinner as you climb higher, you see less and less people, and the weather is relentless. The elements, as in life, will test your commitment as a leader. Near the summit of Everest, the temperature on average is -30 degrees and the winds average 100mph. Because the air is so thin, helicopters aren't able to fly up in order to evacuate the stranded or injured. For the most part, if you don't come down on your own, you become a part of the mountain.

What does that say about the ones that still go? It says they are full of life, and they must have a purpose for doing what they're doing, egotistical or not. Leadership will always require you to climb up, but like Everest, there are moments when leadership means cutting dead weight off. If two climbers commit to the summit together, once past a certain point, the other won't have the strength the save his/her friend. When you commit...you commit! Too often in various forms of leadership and life, people are trying to drag dead weight individuals to the top. You don't have the time to do that, and in doing so you actually do harm to your team and yourself. I know they're your friend, but if they signed on the dotted line, its game on.

You're not operating at your best because you're busy trying to get others to commit. If they won't commit without you constantly pressing the fact, they're probably not going to commit at all. Just face it, but remember that you're not excluded from that fact. Commitment takes personal revelation, and once again, that comes from purpose and vision. If you want your team to follow your example of commitment, make sure they understand the first two principles, and make sure that they know you're willing to lay down a part of your life for them. That means letting your ego die on the mountain, letting your pride die on the mountain, letting your assumptive and indirect nature die on the mountain. Why? You can't carry extra weight up the mountain and lead your team at the same time. You've got to look inside yourself and figure out what's holding you down, and holding you back. Cut the dead weight, and shield them from the loss of a good leader that did too much with too little.

## *Free Game*

Commitment is deeper than just showing up every day. It's about being intentional and growing in life. You can be physically present, and totally absent at the same time.

### **3 Things That Signify Commitment In A Good Leader**

1. Self-Motivated and Needs Little Supervision

2. Fight To Function Under Stress
3. Self-Evaluate

If you constantly need someone to root for you, and pump you up to get something done, you're not going to be able to sustain victory over a long period of time. Here's the deal though, being motivated, when it comes to leadership, has nothing to do with how you feel that day. I'll say it again, it has nothing to do with your personal feelings about your day, how things did or did not go, or what tomorrow might bring. Your feelings are always on the move, that's why they are called "E – Motions."

Not to mention, all of your feelings originate within your own mind. That means that nobody can make you feel anything, it's all in how you perceive it. So, the next time you get bent out of shape about something, check your source first before pointing the finger. If you're truly committed, you'll fight the funk and work your way out. You know what I mean when I say, 'The Funk'. When you wake up in the morning and nothing bad happened, but you're already frustrated with the day.

You're wearing a natural frown and you know it, but you don't care to change it. It's the kind of day where if somebody said the wrong thing, for whatever reason, you just might end up in jail. Even though you have a clean criminal record, ha-ha. The funk is real man! It's sneaky though, and sucks the life out of you. On that day you feel like the worst student, the worst parent, the worst spouse, the worst significant other...the worst human. It feels like the world is against you, even though 9/10 times its just you making stuff up in your head because you slept the wrong way and had a cramp in your neck the whole night. Or, on a real note, you never decompressed from the day before. If you go to sleep fresh off your phone, frustrated and the like, you're literally carrying yesterday into your tomorrow.

Those are the times when leaders have to show up. We all experience that mystery monster emotion when things just feel like a crumbling wall all around you. What you do in the middle of the funk, greatly determines what type of a leader you are. Are you the enduring leader, or the part time leader? Can you still empower others in the middle of your own storm and remain steady, or do you excuse yourself from the role and act out of character all day? It's got nothing whatsoever to do with perfection, and everything to do with the process. Now, if you can perfect the process, then you're on to something. The strong leader is able to do a quick self-assessment, control their emotional state, and make a decision to break out of the fog. A weak person in a leadership position will do the opposite under pressure. They will consistently complain, drift into an emotional coma, and then be frustrated with themselves after everything passes over because they know they could've, and should've done better. Consistency requires conscious decisions!

**Check The Default**

When a child falls and scrapes their knee, their natural response is to cry and look for immediate support. At the time, the child, for all intents and purposes, is a follower. As that child grows up into their teenage or young adult years, things change. If that same young person, now simply being older, fell and scraped their knee, most would acknowledge the pain with the classic 'inhaling teeth suck'. You know what I'm talking about, don't play dumb. When it's painful but not excruciating, or how about this one? When you put rubbing alcohol on a paper cut. It's as if you're trying to fake smile, and breathe simultaneously without opening your mouth. You get the picture now. So, you do that, you grunt, you laugh while jogging it off, or for you heathens...you cuss, ha-ha.

Either way, at the age of 19, you don't cry uncontrollably and scream for a loved one when you scuff your knee. Well, hopefully! But, the point is this, you will always default to what comes natural to you, or what you've been taught. As a child, you cry and look for help, but as a young adult, you assess the injury and decide based on the severity of the wound.

Leaders must check their defaults if they're going to remain consistent and committed. What do you do in the middle of an employment drought? What happens to your structure when you fail the test you had studied so hard for? How do you respond when you aren't admitted into the school of your dreams? What do you default to?

When it comes to commitment, you may have to reprogram the way you think, but it will prove to be rewarding later in life. Remember, just because you've been doing something a certain way your whole life, that doesn't mean you were doing it right in the first place. Leaders know that part of commitment, ironically, is change. Those unwilling to change, even when doing something the wrong way, are unfit to lead. They are committed, but committed to themselves and not the mission. If you refuse to check your defaults under pressure, it's most likely because you're afraid of what will come to the surface. I will tell you this, awareness of issue, without action is a waste. When assessing your commitment level, make sure you assess yourself, and your role at the same time, so that your commitment level will remain without question. In the end, you want your default to put you in a position to dominate your situation.

### *Free Game*

The length of each person's journey is different. Therefore, consistency for you, may not be the same as consistency for me. As a leader, it might take me 8 years to lock down something that you acquired in 2 years. Don't be frustrated with other people's speed. Some of them are skipping steps and jumping line. You'll see who earned the prize in the end. Don't look at somebody else's timeline, that's not your business.

**Culture Of Commitment**

Commitment is literally all around us. When you get married, they ask you a question. "Do you take this person to be your lawfully wedded husband, or wife?" If, and when you do, they announce you as being joined together. When you buy a car, they give you a contract that you sign, saying that you are committed to being the owner of this vehicle. When you're at a local swimming pool standing in line for the diving board, there is an implied assumption that you are committed to climbing the ladder and diving when your turn comes. Commitment is everywhere. Here's the thing though, you can commit to the wrong stuff. You have to be very careful as a leader, what you commit yourself to. A giant in the mental health industry, and big brother mentor of mine, Roderick Brown, said that we must always be aware of our habits. He said, "You will always develop habits, they aren't going away. The trick is to make sure the bad habits that you consistently display are replaced with good ones that help you and don't hurt you."

Did you hear that? Wow! We all have habits. Habits are things that we do consistently, even if that consistency is stretched over a period of time. The challenge that so many of us have is that we hold on to things that we need to let go of. We major in the minors and minor in the majors. If you know that your internal peace tends to drop right before bed, you need to look at what you're doing before you go to sleep. If you realize that you are on your cell phone reading up on politics, you've obviously developed a habit. While that habit may keep you up to date on things, it's also costing you more than you're really gaining in the long run. Instead, try reading something peaceful before bed, or looking at the political polls at least three hours before bed time. You're still developing a habit, just a habit that serves you and doesn't hurt you. So, check your habits people. One massive, and I mean colossal flaw that I've discovered as it relates to commitment is when leaders overcommit. You can be doing the right thing too much if you're not careful. Often times, it's the ones that have the right heart, and want to do the right thing, but they suck at saying, "No!" For several reasons, some people struggle so hard to decline an offer. They feel as if they are letting others down when they don't accept every offer. Let me tell you something. You are letting others down when you run yourself into the ground by refusing to say, NO!

This is a point that you really need to pay attention to, because a lot of leaders burn themselves out trying to keep up with ridiculous expectations. Many people simply have low self-esteem, and a poor self-image, so they spend all of their time people pleasing. As a leader, you have to learn to say, "No." It doesn't make you a bad person, it shows that you are responsible. When you have committed to excellence, you can't agree to do everything, because you just don't have the capacity to deliver your best while being stretched so thin. You'd be surprised how often people think they are just inherently bad leaders, only to find out that it was really a matter of them having their hands in too many things at one time.

If we don't take the time to deal with our attitudes, then it will be hard to appreciate the accolades. I want you to really think about your level of commitment. I want you to seriously consider if your actions back up your statements. It's so easy to talk a big game and put on a good show in front of people, but when all of your resources and support falls away, who are you? What did you promise to, "You?" Remember, defaulting is a completely normal thing in life. We all default and naturally gravitate towards one thing or another. I just want you to be sure that you are being pulled, or pulling yourself in the right direction.

So, here's a few questions I want you to answer in regards to commitment:

- Do you have an issue with commitment? This is not limited to work, or school; I mean anywhere?

_____

_____

- If so, where did it come from? This could be past trauma, experiences, relationships, jobs, school, etc.

_____

_____

- How are you working to grow out of that issue?

_____

_____

- Do you ever find yourself over committing, and saying, "Yes," to everything? If so, why?

### Is It Stupid, Or Do You Quit Too Much?

As a leader, commitment is non-negotiable. The purpose and drive will determine how you see things, and therefore, how locked in you are to achieving your goal. In high school, I struggled with math. I just couldn't figure out the formulas, no matter how hard I tried. While we all have different strengths within the field of education, I can honestly say that while I worked hard, I had a lot left in the tank. It was easier for me to just say that math was stupid though, because it gave me an emergency exit. It was more convenient for me to just say, "Out of sight, out of mind", even though it was in my face every day. I would say things to myself like, "Math is just a waste of time. Those kids obviously are smarter than me, and that's ok because I'm going to the military anyway." As if they don't use mathematical equations in combat.

What I was really doing was trying to protect myself. Because I was so insecure, I didn't want to be seen, nor view myself as a failure. As a defense mechanism, I labeled math as being the problem, instead of me. Naturally, that made no sense, because it was the same class that was being taught to millions of students nationwide, and worldwide for that matter. But, I couldn't ask for help, right? If I did, people would see that I didn't know what to do, and that would tarnish my coveted high school reputation of being a simple guy that ran track, and kept to himself. Oh goodness, I couldn't imagine what would have happened if I had asked for help, dominated math, and became a class leader. It would have been so terrible if girls started flocking to me like a moth to a flame because I was both athletic and super intelligent. I hope you hear the sarcasm in my voice, because that's not what happened.

No, instead, I struggled with math and barely passed because I wanted to save face in front of people that I don't even talk to, and barely remember today. What was my consistency and commitment like though? I worked hard honestly, but it wasn't as hard as I could work. What about you? Are you working hard, or hardly working? You know your standard and ability. You know how to hide the gas level meter in your work ethic. Some of us are three quarters full and we're acting like we're running on fumes. Question...is that situation just stupid, or are you just quitting and taking the easy way out? Shielding yourself from the truth will never shield you from reality, so just commit already.

## **Your Perceived Max Is Your Minimum**

Former Navy SEAL, David Goggins said, "When most people think they're at 100%, they're really only at about 40% of their true ability." I remember hearing Goggins talk about a concept he calls, "Callousing The Mind." What this relentless commando described was how you have to harden the soft places in your mentality that urge you to quit when hardship comes. He said that we need to get a mental state where our excuses know they're in trouble. He broke down how facing your fears was the only way to truly find freedom, and I agreed. Freedom is found in the fight, and my wife is a shining example.

My wife decided that she was going to have our third child with no medical assistance, as in a natural birth with no medications. I remember telling her how amazing she was, how strong, how courageous, how beautiful and powerful she looked. Between the two of us, we hadn't slept in twenty-four hours legitimately when it was game on. We showed up at the hospital and she was already having heavy contractions.

They took her to the back for monitoring before they called me into the room. Then the marathon started. Although the entire laboring process was only about 6 hours, it felt like 12. I remember going in excited to be my wife's assistant and support. Without having eaten in 9 hours and awake for 19 at the time, my body was exhausted. There were so many times when I wanted to just sit down and rest, but every time I thought about relaxing, I remembered why I was there. I was committed to my wife, and my soon to be newborn son.

With every hour, I grew more and more tired. At one point, I was so wiped out that I felt nauseous and almost threw up. My body was telling me to lay down, but my mind kept telling me, "You got more in the tank." I started getting light headed, so I took a seat near her as she soldiered on through the early morning hours. My feet hurt, eyes were closing, and my upper legs were worn out from standing and squatting all night. We had so many little things to do that it seemed as if we weren't even making a dent. I looked at my wife and said, "Honey, everything has a finish line...cross it!"

In that moment, my fatigue began to fade. It was time to lock it in. I got my second wind, and then my third, fourth, fifth, sixth, and seventh. It took that many to get through the night and be the support system that my wife needed. I never thought about quitting, but my body did. I was committed though. If I didn't hold the line, who would? If I didn't stay focused, things might slip through the cracks. If I didn't take control, I would've become unraveled.

Remember though, I'm not the hero here. Take everything I just said, multiply it by "Heck No," divide it by "Good Lord," and then add "There Is No Way In... You Know What," and that's what my wife went through. By the way, she nailed it with no medications. Our third child was born healthy and happy, Praise God! Why share that story though? Well, as the father, I could only be supportive as much as humanly possible. For my wife, she had to be 10000% committed from the very beginning, because she would be carrying our child. She would be delivering him, and going through tremendous pain. She would be feeding him in the middle of the night, unless other accommodations were made for me to help. She was phenomenal, and at her best that day. She had to be absolutely committed, and so do you.

Here's a few questions for you to think about:

- As an individual and a leader, what qualities have you not given birth to yet? Are you as focused, healthy, wealthy, peaceful, grateful, etc., as you want to be?

- What will you do the next time your mind says, "We can quit, it's only going to hurt us?" What will you do when you devalue yourself as if you don't matter?

- When hard times come, do you recall the truth that all things must come to an end, good and bad?

## Shield Over Spear Summary

Team members everywhere are already familiarized with the concept of quitting. It's nothing personal, but quitting holds you in place, and testifies of weakness. Some of you may not like that statement, I understand, but it doesn't take you out of the spotlight. What most team members are thirsty for, is a committed leader that won't back down when things get tough. When your team knows that you are committed to the mission, and that you are committed to them, the sky is the limit. Stop settling for second best, pick up your shield, and keep moving until you discover what's on the other side of that wall. It takes guts to be committed, but it takes a strong human being to tackle the next battle phase...OWNERSHIP!

# Principle 4: Ownership

*Freeing yourself was one thing; taking ownership of that freed self is another.*

**-Toni Morrison**

## Ownership, it's legally being in possession of, and taking control of the results.

On the battlefield of Thermopylae, each soldier took ownership of their role in the fight. They never looked to their brother, and pointed the finger. There are two words that come to mind when I think of how they operated. Awareness & Action! You see, it does no good for a leader to see the problem and assume that someone else will take care of it. Instead, leaders see the issues before them, and respond accordingly. When soldiers approached, men stepped forward to meet them without question. If help was needed, help was given without question. This chapter is going to be particularly difficult for many of you when it comes to leadership and personal development, because this requires direct accountability. When I say direct, I mean direct.

## No Punches Pulled

Some people are liars, straight up. We like the "IDEA" of things, but the follow through and accountability is a ghost in reality. We smooth talk people into thinking that we're going to do this or that, even when we know we aren't. The biggest lie of all time is when we tell ourselves that garbage. "I'm going to really do it this time," we tell ourselves. Yeah, right. Now, I'm not one to put people down, because I was guilty of the same thing in the past. I had to come to terms with my truth though, look at myself in the mirror, and call it for what it was...crap!

We think that integrity and character only applies to how we treat other people. No! Your integrity and character can be absolute turtle crap if you're constantly lying to yourself. You are 'other people.' You are a person too. You're no better off being straight and committed with the rest of the world, only to shortchange yourself. You have value too. So, you have to put all your cards on the table and stop playing the game. Face the music, no matter what the tune may be. If you can't look at yourself and take complete ownership of your response to what life has thrown at you, that's your fault. Let's make something clear though, not everything in life, good or bad, was your doing. However, your comeback is always going to be your responsibility. If you want to grow in life, you need to get in the closet with that deceptive monster and knock that punk out.

## **The Shield Of Trust**

I'll never forget learning how to clear a building with a team of four during an active shooter training I participated in. This of course was when I was a police officer, ha-ha. I'm not some hyperactive vigilante citizen, gee-wizz. Anyway, we had initially used a method called, the diamond. In this particular method, you move like the base pattern on a baseball field. Hopefully you get the picture, but if not, think of it like a compass pointing north, south, east and west. Then we moved to a Rolling-T, which basically allowed us to cover a hallway or an open space while moving forward with all directions in view.

I remember being assigned to a team with three officers I hadn't worked with before. Naturally, I was a little hesitant because I had typically done well in scenario-based training, and I didn't want my team to look bad. Here's the truth though, I didn't care about how the team looked at all. I cared 100% about how I looked, I didn't want to look bad. Have you ever experienced or acted like that? Well if you raised your hand, you were wrong. Leaders don't act like that. It just reminded me, at the time, I wasn't being a leader at all. Everything I did was in my best interest alone. How much of a contradiction is that? It's actually embarrassing.

There I was, a police officer that had sworn to protect citizens, and others serving alongside me, and all I could think about was myself. Some of you may not get the correlation, but how you do small things is how you do big things too. How was I going to keep an open heart for the public that I served if I was complaining and crying like a three-year-old because I didn't get the play buddies I wanted? Come on!

In the moment, I really got frustrated though, when I saw one of the officers assigned to my group. He did not have a good reputation as being tactical, knowledgeable, or even prepared, when it came to the profession. I was hoping to be switched, but my number was up, and I led my team in. We ran into the building together, formed up, and proceeded to move down the hallway. One of the instructors was role playing, and lobbed bead filled pipe bombs straight at us. My automatic inclination was to move back, but I heard an instructor yell at us, "Move back, and you're dead," so we jumped over it and pushed on. The entire time I kept thinking to myself, "If this is tough for me, the rest of my team is barely functioning I'm sure." I only had one bad partner that day... my Ego!

Within a matter of seconds, we were facing role players acting as school shooters. It was intense! Gunfire sounds coming from different directions, student role players screaming as they ran down the halls with their hands in the air, and so much more. All of these things were just training for the horrible incidents that take place in this country every year. We were training for what we knew could possibly happen one day. A role player was up ahead of me, and appeared to have a weapon. As the point man, my job was to keep eyes on everything in front, and communicate that back to the team. As the role player entered the room, I yelled out, "Contact Front...Contact Front!" My team and I then moved to the room and prepared to make entry.

We issued commands for the role player to surrender, but it was to no avail. We then made entry into the room. We used a sweeping technique called, "Slicing the Pie", which allowed you to visually clear an open room in segments, so as not to miss or overlook a threat. Here was the rule though. When you entered the room, and proceeded to your position, you were responsible for whatever was in your scope of view. On that day, I assumed that my team would struggle with this exercise, so after visually clearing my area, I proceeded to keep my weapon ahead of me, but scanned the rest of the room to make sure they didn't miss anything as they brought up the rear.

Just as my eyes were coming back to my assigned zone, "Bang," out jumped the role player. I was caught, and my team now had to worry about carrying me out of the room while addressing a lethal opponent, and hopefully getting me medical assistance before I expired. Again, this was role playing, but it's obviously a mistake I might have made in real life. A mistake that was unacceptable.

Here's the takeaway. As the point man, or the one in the center, I was not responsible for what was besides, or behind me, at all! As a matter of fact, if there was a threat ahead of me, and a threat behind me, I put my team in danger by not owning the direction that I was assigned to. In my arrogance of wanting to look good, I jeopardized my own life, the life of my team, and the life of the students, if that had been a real incident. The next step was for me to own it. My good friend happened to be one of the instructors, he was on the SWAT Team. "Dude, what the heck was that?" he asked. "That was my mistake man, sorry," I responded. "No crap it was your fault. What were you thinking? You know how to clear a room; you've done it a hundred times," he reminded me. "I know, I just didn't think my team was in control of their assignment," I told him. "So, you end up costing us a man, and more, huh?" he stated. I shook my head. "Run it back, and get it right!" he told me, as we regathered.

I apologized to my team, and we went back through the scene, but this time we were flawless. As a matter of fact, the officer that didn't have the best of reputations said, "Man, when I got assigned to your group, I knew we were going to dominate. I was surprised when you let that guy sneak up on you." I had to own it in that moment. "Man, that was my fault, and I apologize. I didn't trust you guys, and I assumed one of you would mess up, so I tried to cover the whole room myself" I said. "Hey, we understand that we can't all be Superman like you, but we've got your back, and we know you have ours too," one officer said. I learned in that moment, that ownership and trust were connected.

If I owned, and I mean completely owned, my assignment then I freed up the other three officers to focus on their assignments. By all of us owning our individual assignments, we then became a free-flowing force that would be tremendously difficult to beat. You see, people need to be able to trust that you will do what you say you're going to do. They should be able to rest comfortably knowing that something valuable is in your hands. They should be able to sleep at night on the battlefield, because they know that you are standing guard over them.

Trust is always linked to ownership, as fear is always linked to ego. The person that carries their resume on their shoulders is the one that I don't want to be in the room with, because I know what they're thinking. They're thinking only about themselves. In all honesty, can your team, family or friends trust you?

Here's the deal. Trust is something that is earned, not freely given, but it does require taking a chance. In taking a chance, they are actually giving you a trial run of their trust. There isn't great expectation in the trial run, because the purpose is to help the person gauge the likelihood of a particular result. If you go on a date with someone you meet, you're extending a small amount of trust that they won't embarrass you, start screaming at the dinner table, steal candy at the movies, and so on. But, you never know. So, you extend that graceful amount of trust in order to see how they treat what you've given them, and from there you can determine to what extent you give them access to your life.

In leadership, as the one in charge, you build the culture of trust in your group or program. You have to take ownership of the trust factor by letting those under your command know that you have their back.

Here's a couple of things you can do to build trust, and embed the trust factor into your team:

- **Recognize that some people don't know how to trust easily because of past experiences**: This is difficult for some leaders, especially those that were fortunate enough to come from a well-established and trusting environment. As a leader, you have to empathize with your team and give clarity in regards to what you're trying to build, because not everybody came up like you did.

- **Explain why you want to build a trusting atmosphere, what the benefits are, and what you are

**going to personally do in order to lay that foundation**: People don't care about big words and empty promises. People want to know that when the dust settles, the people that said they would be there, will be there.

- **Start small and don't make promises you can't keep**: One of the biggest mistakes that leaders make, especially new ones, is that they bite off more than they can chew. It's great to have a grand vision for the present and future, but you want to make sure that you can follow through on what you say you're going to do. I don't care if it's letting somebody borrow a pencil in class, or sending an email for follow up. Keeping your word in the small things is just as important as following through on the big things.

- **Hold loosely to the picture**: Just be aware that not everything is going to turn out the way you want it to on the first try every time. People get discouraged and want to quit too quickly. If there was never a challenge, how would you truly learn what you're capable of in life? When this happens, you shouldn't just give up and say that it was a big waste of time. Instead, revisit your approach and move from there.

- **Execute**: One of the best ways to establish trust is to just do more and talk less. Results speak for themselves. So, as a leader, you have to know how to gauge your own trust meter, and assign things to your team that will foster their growth, while you crush it on your end too. When you just get out and do it, there isn't much else that needs to be said.

## *Free Game*

Ownership isn't free, it's going to cost you something! Every time, and every day, it will be costly. Yet, it will be worth it. Ownership is best friends with leadership!

### **Rambo, Predator, Commando, and the Gas Station Rooftop**

When I was younger, I lived in Kalamazoo, Michigan. Yes, it's a real place. Although the city name sounds silly, there was always plenty to do. Our house was right next to a huge field, and a closed down gas station. The only thing separating my yard, and the field lot was a chain linked fence. At the time, my best friend's name was Roman. We were as thick as thieves, you might say, even though we didn't steal. One thing we did a lot, besides play outside, was watch action movies.

Our favorite movies then consisted of Predator and Commando, starring Arnold Schwarzenegger, and Rambo, starring Sylvester Stallone. All three movies were all about setting traps, destroying the enemy, and accomplishing impossible missions. Let's just say, we had big imaginations at the time, and we found ourselves in the imaginary jungles of the Amazon facing a tyrant war lord. You already know where this is going. Our mission was simple. We had to scale the compound walls (abandoned gas station), and throw grenades from the rooftop into the paths of the enemy convoys.

So, we climbed up the back of the gas station using an old rusty pipe. Once in place, we glanced over the rooftop at the enemy patrol units speeding by. Again, some of you already know where this is going. We then pulled out a handful of grenades, and proceeded to yank the imaginary pins as we threw them onto the enemy roadway. "Direct Hit!" There was only one problem. Well, actually there were a lot of problems. Here's just a few of them, ha-ha. We weren't soldiers, the compound was a gas station, the enemy supply trucks were citizens on a busy street, and the grenades we had were pockets full of rocks.

So, needless to say, the enemy associates across the road, also known as, the Burger King employees, called the police on us. Here's where it gets interesting! The officer pulled up at like 60mph, as if we were robbing a bank. We freaked out, and wanted to instinctively run. There was one problem though. A 14ft high problem to be exact, because we were on the roof of a building. The officer jumped out of his car and yelled, "FREEZE!" as if we were going to listen to a man screaming with his hand on his gun. I told Roman, "We gotta jump now!" Roman was terrified though, and just couldn't do it.

So, I did what any imaginary soldier would do, I jumped! Yes, I ran to the edge and dropped 14ft to the ground just as the officer was turning the corner. He yelled for me to stop, but he obviously didn't know I was related to Speedy Gonzalez, the beloved mouse from my Looney Tunes days. I kicked it into high gear, and the officer ate my dust.

The next issue came at me pretty quickly. I lived next door! So, I ran in the house while my dad was sleeping, opened the garage door, and threw a bunch of balls, skateboards and such into the front yard. This was of course, after I changed shirts. Minutes later, the police officer turned into my driveway with Roman in the backseat crying like a baby. The officer got out, and I acted like a totally polite stranger. I think everything happened so fast that he couldn't tell if it was me or not, and I had switched shirts. Not to mention, nobody in their right mind would be so dumb as to run from the cops right next door to their house, right? Wrong! The officer walked past me with a confused look on his face and knocked on the door. My dad woke up from his nap, and answered it.

By then, I was laughing, because I knew two things the officer didn't: 1) My dad had no clue what was going on, and 2) My dad did not like police officers at all.

After my dad, half awake, basically told the officer to get off his property, he did just that, and took Roman home. Now, Roman's dad was a preacher, and a good man, but Mr. Frank didn't play games, and would whoop us in a heartbeat. Roman didn't sit down on the bus the next day, and I laughed because I had gotten away with it, and he didn't. "That's what you get for telling," I said. But, I was the one in the wrong. I was the one that left Roman behind, and didn't own up to what we did together. I was the one that left him to take the full blame. I was the real loser here. Roman, if you're reading this, just know that, "I'm sorry!" I'm sorry that you didn't listen to me, and jump when I told you to boy! You wouldn't have gotten that whooping if you had just listened! Ha-ha! Love You Bro!

There was an element of personal ownership that I was lacking, even at such a young age. It didn't matter if it was something petty, or something big. I never should have left my friend on that rooftop, as funny as it is looking back now, of course. I wasn't leading, I was only seeking to save myself.

I assumed that Roman had the same mindset and heart to escape that I did at the time. The moment I saw him frozen, I should have stayed. If he was frozen, it was my job to thaw him out with the warmth of our brotherhood. He should have known that I had his back, no matter what. Truthfully, I'm ashamed of myself for leaving him. Anything could have happened, and there would have been nobody to account for, or discount the incident. But, that's what happens when crap hits the fan, we default to personal preservation, and we cast off all allegiance to those we should protect.

Did both of us make the decision to climb that rooftop and throw rocks? Yes! But, it was my idea. From the jump, I was responsible. The only thing I was attacking at the moment was my own personal plan of escape, all the while leaving my very best brother in the hands of an officer that had almost pulled a gun on me. Listen, fear will always tell you what you shouldn't do, but courage will tell you what you must! In that moment, if I could change one thing, it would have been my priority list. When I tell you that Roman to this day is still my brother, that's my brother! And I left him, like a coward. I took no ownership of our relationship and I prioritized what I wanted, and not what was truly worth sacrificing for.

What about you? Was there ever a time when you left somebody alone on a thing that you had just as much a hand in as them? Can you recall a time when you knew that you were obligated to take ownership of the incident, but you fled, denied, or ignored the truth? How did you feel? Why did you do it?

Most of all, have you changed your ways? If not, why? If so, what was the spark to become a stronger person?

_____

_____

_____

_____

_____

_____

Honestly though, some of you might be saying, "K.D. do you really expect an 11-year-old to understand sacrifice, and ownership under pressure?" The answer is, "YES...I DO!" I'll tell you why. There was a story about a family during the Holocaust. The mother and father had been taken away by the Nazis, and there were three children left behind. One boy, around 9 or 10 years old, and his two younger sisters that were around 7, and 5. The children did their best to hide, and get out of town before being caught, but unfortunately that didn't happen. The coward Nazis rummaged through the house where the children were hiding, until they heard a sound.

As the heartless men moved closer to their hiding place, the older brother knew he had to do something. So, he tucked his sisters away after telling them that he loved them, and ran out of the house making as much noise as possible. The spineless weaklings chased the boy outside as he drew attention away from his sisters. They shot him in the street, and left him for dead. The sisters escaped, because a little boy refused to quit on his siblings. He took complete and total ownership of their safety, down to the point of giving his life for them. So, yes...I expect them to understand. The question is, do you?

## *Free Game*

Leaders have internal mirrors everywhere. They are constantly looking to improve, and therefore welcome their reflection.

Poor authority figures, I won't call them leaders, reject their reflection unless it fits the image they desire. If they don't see what they want to see, they find a way to manipulate the mirror, put its faults on display, or justify the picture of a person they see. They are afraid, without a doubt.

But, real leaders love the mirror. They stay in the mirror, and not in a "Light Skinned...I know I'm hot" kind of way, ha-ha. No, they're aware that whatever remains in the dark will only allow poisonous seeds to grow. Yes, darkness has a perverted light that allows things to fester and spring up too. So, you have to be on guard for those things that you don't want to deal with. If you don't deal with them now, they will force you to deal with them later. Good leaders though...they realize that insecurities come from pride, and opinion. They know that strength comes from acceptance, and correction. Michael Jackson said it best, "I'm starting with the man in the mirror!"

**If You Wait, You're Too Late**

A lot of people work really hard while their boss or coworkers are around, but not because they care about producing good results for the group. I see this everywhere, and truth be told, it's engrained in us as humans. When we were kids, and our parents told us to clean up the house, what did we do? Many of us just chilled out until we heard the cars pulling up in the driveway, or if our parents were home, we made a lot of noise in the other room to make it seem like we were really getting after it, even though we know we weren't doing jack squat. Isn't it ridiculous that we can get more done in five stressful minutes than we can in five complacent hours?

No matter what level of leadership you hold, you always want to be in the mindset of working to win. That means that it doesn't matter who is around, what day it is, or what anyone else has to say, you don't wait...you dominate. If you're one of those people that has convinced yourself that you work better under pressure, you're just not disciplined. What you're really doing is waiting until the last minute so that your mind responds to panic, and forces you to respond. If you have to be forced, you're showing a sign of weakness.

Here are some reasons why you shouldn't wait until the last minute, or only operate when directly supervised:

- Unknown Events And Variables: There are so many things that you cannot take account for in life. You don't know the weather for certain, whether you're going to be in a wreck, if you'll fall ill, if you'll be robbed, lose your keys, or your printer breaks down. These are all of the unknowns that you gamble with by attempting to work hard when the deadline is approaching.

- Pride: You're assuming that you can master everything on the spot, and that everything will go as it always has. I'm telling you, one day your card will get pulled and you're going to fall terribly hard on your face. You're going to wish that you were a little humbler, and a little more understanding. But, when it happens, don't say I didn't warn you.

- Discipline Is Lacking: When you have the opportunity to plan for an assignment, event, program, or venture...do it. Sure, working on a final term paper at the beginning of the semester sounds a bit ridiculous. You know what doesn't sound stupid though? Starting your outline at the beginning of the semester, adding another piece to the puzzle every week so it's fresh on your mind, and when everybody else is scrambling to get their thoughts together...you're five months ahead.

- <u>Poor Example:</u> Here's a question that I often ask myself. If others were following my example, would they most likely succeed or fail? Now, I know that's a bit subjective because people vary in many ways, but in the grand scheme of things...are you leading well? We can go back and forth about what's right and what's wrong, but it's all just semantics. In the end, can they look to you for guidance through life example or not?

## **Moving Like The Master**

In the movie, Troy, starring Brad Pitt as Achilles, there was a particular moment that caught my eye. Know this, Achilles was the man! Achilles had a cousin named, Patroclus. Patroclus had followed Achilles to the war in Troy. The king of Troy's son, Hector, was a valiant warrior, and wanted nothing more than to face Achilles himself. Achilles ordered his men not to fight in the next day's battle, but as the Trojans attacked, so did Achilles, and his men. Or, so they thought. Hector met who he had believed to be Achilles on the battlefield, and after a few swift moves, he killed him. The unbeatable Achilles was dead. Again, so they thought.

That is, until his helmet, and armor were removed, only to realize that it was Patroclus wearing the armor of Achilles all along. When the fighting stopped, and the men returned to camp, Achilles came out of his tent and found his men laying down their weapons. He questioned his captain on whether or not he disobeyed his direct order? The captain told him, "We thought it was you. He wore your armor, and even moved like you!"

Achilles was furious! He began to choke his captain, in a fit of rage over his cousin's death. He was angry with everyone...except himself! He was angry with Patroclus for challenging Hector. He was angry at his captain for disobeying his orders, and he was furious with Hector for killing his cousin. Again though, he was never upset with himself. After all, as the leader, it's his responsibility to know his men's whereabouts. It's up to him to train his men to follow his rule by face, and not assumed command. And, it is his responsibility to guard his own armor. If those things had been done, Patroclus wouldn't have died. It's a matter once again, of ownership!

Poor leaders will always find a way to pass the blame. This is often done because they know they screwed up. So, in order to save face and still assert their perception of dominance, they point the finger and say, "Look...there is our problem!" Lack of personal accountability is not just costly for the one that permits it, but also for those close to them.

### *Free Game*

Do you tend to take ownership of your mistakes? Even greater, do you step into the next level of supreme responsibility, and look at how you could have helped someone else make better decisions? If not? Why? Leadership is about influencing others for the good of the cause. Keep in mind... "That isn't my problem!" is not a sufficient answer. If something affects your mission in any way, it just became your problem! So, how do you operate?

_____

_____

_____

Lack of ownership is really a battle with one thing...PRIDE! If a person is able to put their selfish personal interest aside, and realize that a whole perspective on self-interest is better, then things can change. What do I mean by that? A selfish person only sees the bad that can happen in a situation, and how they will be looked at in light of that thing. A CEO may not take the time to have a good conversation with the building's custodian, because he/she may feel they are more valuable than the building employee. They may not want to be seen with a person that cleans the building. Instead, they would prefer to be seen with the CFO, or some great investor. Why? Because it makes them look better, and it feeds their unquenchably narcissistic ego. In the end, people like that can only see what's best for one person...themselves.

Now, what if that same CEO prided him/herself in being completely intentional when speaking to people? What if they were known for going out of their way to make sure the elevator attendant, custodians, etc. all felt appreciated and valued? What if that CEO was known for encouraging, and empowering his/her employees to go back to school, pursue more in life, and never to give up on their dreams?

What if they saw the value in relationships that lasted, rather than superficial associates that make them look good for a single meeting? Which would you prefer to work for, the CEO that only wanted to be seen with big money lenders, or the CEO that won't leave the building until he/she shakes the hand of the front desk worker? Now, which one are you more associated with by how you conduct yourself?

That's what leadership is all about. That is what Shield Over Spear, means to the core. It means you place your shield out front because you're in a fight against societal norms, peer pressure and outside influence. It means that you utilize both offense and defense to keep your team, and yourself flowing. It's guarding your squad, and others from destructive habits that only benefit one, instead of many. It's looking at a situation and saying, "I got this, so that they can..." It's not about arrogance, or overconfidence...it's about serving the person next to you and getting the job done.

## Leaders Own What Most Would Rather Run From

When I was an officer, I remember the first suicide call I was dispatched to. On the way there I was trying to process in my mind what I was about to experience. I had to settle in on the truth that I was going to become very familiar with this tragic event. I recall not wanting to go, and hoping that someone else would take the call because they were closer. Sure enough, the radio chirped up.

"Hey this is 214, I'll take that suicide call. I'm not far out," the officer said to the radio dispatcher. Internally I was so grateful. I wanted to go, because I knew I would have to face it one day. I just didn't want to be in charge. Then my training officer grabbed the radio and shouted out, "Negative dispatch...we'll take it for training!" "COME ON!," is all I could say in my mind, but I knew I needed to go, so I continued on.

You know, the police academy lasted for almost half of a year, for five of the seven weekdays straight through, and tough at that. But, no matter how much training you have, there are some things you just can't prepare for. Some things you just have to deal with. My training coach had been on many of them, and it didn't seem to bother him that much, but not me. It messed with me big time. I'm a man of faith, and as such, my hope is, and will always be for people to know how much God loves them.

This particular day took me to a place that I was unfamiliar with in my heart. The reality that someone was so weighted down by the pain of this world that they believed it was better to die. It was heartbreaking, and still is. If you're reading this, and you have battled with depression to the point of considering death...think again! We need you, and what you have to offer the world can only come from you. I can't take your place, and you can't take mine. No matter what it takes...FIGHT! Fight to stay above the water, even if you have been swimming in tough seas for what seems like forever. The land is there, and other people's freedom is locked up in your life. Reach out, don't reach down. You are loved!

Nevertheless, I had a job to do. I recall pulling up to the house. We were the first on scene. I knocked on the door, and a white older woman answered. With her hands shaking over her mouth, she could barely get out any words, but she was able to tell me that her grandson was upstairs. My training coach and I proceeded to climb the staircase, not knowing what we may encounter, we moved quickly and tactically.

As we reached the top of the staircase, I just remember looking into the room on my left. There he was. He was just, there. He had shot himself, and to honor his life, I won't give the details of the scene. I will say, that whatever comes to mind, is probably right. I checked for a pulse, even though I knew it was far too late. My training coach told me to back out of the room so that we could preserve any evidence on the scene. I couldn't move for a minute though, I just stared at his chest. I kept waiting to see him breathe, but he never did. I stood there for what felt like hours, even though it was seconds. I was hoping to be terrifyingly startled with a movement of some kind, but nothing ever happened. He was surely gone. I was at a loss for words and felt numb.

After speaking with the grandmother, and sitting with her on the couch. I experienced one of the worst moments of my life. I heard something that I could not ignore. I heard tires screeching to a halt, and then the cry of a woman. The heart crushing scream...of a mother! She jumped from the car while it was still moving, and came running at the front door yelling to the top of her lungs. My training coach yelled at me, "Don't let her in the door, they're investigating the room now!" I felt helpless. How could I tell a mother that she could not see the man she birthed? What right did I have, even as an officer to deny her the right of one last look? She got to me so fast, and just yelled at me, barely able to breathe, "He needs me!" she said. I just hugged her. From the heart of a son to a mother, in that moment, empathy was my whole world. God knows, I needed help, but I was able to send her outside through the back of the house instead of up the stairs.

It was one of those times I wanted to run away, and be anywhere but there. In those short minutes, I learned to lead. When most people would find an excuse to get off the scene, I stayed, because I knew that it wouldn't be my last time, unfortunately. I was right. But, I owned the scene. I owned the responsibility of providing the best, and most genuine expression of empathy, compassion, and understanding that I could, and more. When the commanding officer arrived, she asked, "Who's scene is this?" And in the midst of terrible tragedy, pain, confusion, and heartache...I stepped forward. "Mine!" I said. "It's mine!" "For what it's worth...good job," she said.

That was one of the first times that I didn't back down from something I would have easily run away from in the past. Is there a time when you had to step into a hard situation? A time that required you to take control, own the scene, and the outcome? If so, what was it like? How did you handle it? What's something you would do different if you could go back? What's something you were proud of yourself for?

_____

_____

_____

_____

_____

_____

*Free Game*

Sometimes, when you feel like giving up, things aren't as bad as they seem. It's how you're looking at the problem that determines if it's even a problem at all or not. Think of it like this. Imagine you're backing out of a parking lot, and you bump into a telephone pole, causing your rear light to bust open. To you, that's a problem, but to a trained auto technician, it's just a quick fix. The problem, and the puzzle are determined by the one with the ability, or inability to address the issue. See the difference?

**Tuck The Strings**

Though we mentioned vision before, I want to look at it from a different perspective. Vision alone, as also previously mentioned, will not produce as much as vision coupled with action. A great leader utilizes the shield of ownership to protect others from unnecessary flare ups from you, the leader. Here's an example. I have an amazing two-year-old son. This dude, is the man...just a little one right now. One thing my son enjoys doing, like any kid, or grown up, is swinging. He loves to swing on low tree branches, he loves to swing on swing sets, and he loves to swing on anything that will hold him up. The problem is, he's two. Therefore, he doesn't know jack squat about weight ratios, particularly in the space of kitchen decor.

In our kitchen we have Faux Wood Blinds. Yes, we're fancy! For those of you that are unfamiliar, those are just what I call, "Country Blinds," where you can pull the left string and they open, or the right one and they close. If you pull both strings at the same time, usually on the far-right side, the entire blind system will raise. Got the picture now? Well, although they came with the house when we bought it, aside from dusting maintenance, they pretty much stay as good as new. That is, unless you have a two-year-old boy attempting to scale the kitchen door, and then repel down using those very tiny, and weak strings. Yes, that's my boy...climbing Mt. Urgonnafall (You're Going To Fall!).

"He's at that age where he's starting to really decide if he wants to listen or not. I mean, it's not a huge surprise because we were all that way around that age. It's just different when you're the parent. Don't get me wrong, he's a phenomenal boy naturally, I mean come on, right? Ha-ha. He does seem to choose the path of most resistance when it comes to certain things though, and I can honestly say that pulling, or attempting to swing from the kitchen blinds counts as one of those things. I found myself tired one day though. It had taken my four-year-old girl, and two-year-old boy, a millennium to come downstairs, and I was furious because we were going to be late for school. I mean, there I was, being an amazing dad, ha-ha, getting breakfast and the works together.

Finally, after his eighty fifth birthday, my two-year-old waltzes into the kitchen smiling. As I'm shuffling around attempting to get everything done, I see him looking at the blinds with a smirk on his face. I gave him the dad stare. You know what I'm talking about. The look that says, "If you do what I know you are thinking about doing, but know you better not do, because I already know what you want to do...I'm gonna snatch you up." He paused, and considered. I went back to making breakfast, only to turn around and see him swinging from the blinds, honestly about to break them. I asked him to stop politely once, and he did...for a millisecond.

Then, as I'm finally finishing up in the kitchen, I see him grab the strings and run in the opposite direction from the door with them in hand. "STOP!" I yelled. By then, I was angry for real, and he could tell. I apologized for yelling, because though he was in the wrong, I should have more self-control as the father, adult, and leader. I noticed that whenever he did that, I would default back to yelling, or have to control my outburst. One day, I had an epiphany. I decided to tuck the flipping strings in the top so he couldn't reach them! Guess what? Problem solved. I didn't have to apologize, because I didn't yell. I didn't yell because I saw the issue with MYSELF, more than I did the issue with him, and I fixed it.

You see, leadership isn't about the person's response as much as it is about yours. Did you hear that? I'll say it again. Life will throw everything at you, but it's up to you to determine what you throw back. I didn't want to be a bad example or father, and at the age of two years old there were far different ways for me to teach him why it's not safe to pull the strings on the blinds. What that situation did though, was offer me an opportunity to own my issues first, while knocking out the thing that was causing it.

So, I challenge you to see the thing that gets under your skin, and pulls you out of character. What's your personal catch? That thing that just makes you want to jump in a volcano. But, instead of attacking your teammate, employee, classmate, or family...attack your reaction! Control your reaction, prevent the problem if possible, and find a better way to communicate what needs to be addressed. In doing so, you will be shielding them, and not harming them with the spear of your words and actions.

What are some triggers that you know you must avoid, or overcome that negatively affect you on a day to day basis?

_____

_____

_____

What are you doing to avoid, or master those triggers?

_____

_____

_____

Here's a few quick things you can do, when you feel like you're on the rise. First, acknowledge that you are in control. If you can deny control, then you'll deny the result of your uncontrolled action. If you take mental control, even if only verbally in the beginning, you will succeed more times than not.

Secondly, identify the root of the issue. Is something really an issue, or an inconvenience? Lastly, decide, and act based on your capacity and willingness to absorb whatever comes after your emotions. If you operate in your emotions, you'll never settle long enough to stand. Emotions are always moving. Settle yourself on the inside, and the rest is easier to regulate.

## Free Game

If you won't be responsible for yourself, you don't deserve to be responsible for anyone else. You know the common saying, "Do unto others as you would have them do unto you?" Well, if you have a leader that is not self-aware and is on the other hand, self-intoxicated, failure is at the doorstep. One of the greatest attributes of any great leader is self-awareness. Self-awareness is not a matter of judgment, as much as it is the ability to see our imperfections, accept them, and still move forward. If you can see the true you, you can make the next move.

### **Shield Over Spear Chapter Summary**

Zero excuses will actually excuse you. There is nothing that will remove you from the mess when it's yours to own. We live in a time when finger pointing is the norm, and accountability is the enemy. I don't want you to think that you have to rule the world, but you do have to rule your world. If you are really going to be a successful leader, you have got to make a decision about your decisions. I'll say it again. You've got to make a decision, about your decisions. You've got to be willing to take the ball, and then keep it in your hands. I've said this a million times, and I'll never stop preaching it... "You aren't responsible for what the world throws at you, but you are 100% in control and responsible for what you throw back!" The best shield that a leader can place in front of their team, is one sealed in ownership, and undergirded with the next step...STRATEGY!

# Principle 5: Strategy

*Every battle is won before it is fought.*

*-Sun Tzu*

**Strategy, is the science and art of command in place to meet opposition in battle under advantageous conditions.**

During the first battle, the mighty king left nothing to chance. It was no accident that they positioned themselves where they did. It was no mistake that the Persians were lured in the way they were. It was no lucky draw, it was strategy. The king, being the leader that he was, had developed a remarkable plan to reduce the enemy's numbers to practically useless accounts. He placed his three hundred warriors in line formations almost thirty rows deep in between two cliffs commonly known as, "The Hot Gates!"

Think of it like this, imagine a small funnel, the kind that you would use to put oil into your car. Now imagine someone holding a fifty-gallon container of oil, and attempting to force it into that tiny funnel. As much pressure as you might think the fifty gallons would produce, one could simply plug the other end of the funnel with your thumb. The only thing that would allow oil to flow through the opposite end would be the fatigue from holding your thumb in place.

That's the precise strategy that the king developed, in order to shield his men from the overwhelming numbers they faced, he put together a plan where he knew that his warrior's strengths would be amplified. So, when the opposing forces met them in the funneled Hot Gates, they learned firsthand what Spartan power felt like. For hours on end, the dominating Spartans literally crushed their opposing forces, to the point where the Persians believed they must have been facing thousands of Spartans and not just the few hundred.

What had the king done though? As a leader, he knew that his men could hold a line, and beat back opposition better than almost any other fighting force on the planet. So, why not use their strength to create an advantage?

It's the same for you! Utilize the strengths and weaknesses that you possess. You heard me right, I said weaknesses too. Why? Your opposition is always going to look for your holes. So, plug them first. Are you creating strategies to minimize your team's weak points, and maximize their strong points? Are you putting them, or yourself, in a position where the odds of winning drastically increases because of the plan you put together? Are you sizing up the thing that would cause you, or them, the most anxiety, stress, or frustration? Have you spent time learning that thing's weaknesses and exploiting it, so that your classmates, squad mates, or employees come into the fight prepared? If not, you're not leading very well. Sun Tzu said, "Let your plans be dark and impenetrable as night, and when you move, fall like a thunderbolt!" Simply put, give yourself the upper hand. If you're just leaving them to the elements, even though you know that you could be of use in the fight, you're not leading...you're managing.

## *Free Game*

Don't overthink things. Almost every person telegraph's their punches. That means that if you watch your opposition long enough, they'll actually tell you when, and how they're going to attack. Everybody slips up. The key is to be patient my friends. A defensive football player, say a cornerback for instance, doesn't watch the wide receiver's hands, or face. No, instead, he watches his hips, and midsection. Why? The legs can't press forward into a run without the hips settling in movement first. It may be a fast movement, but the movement is there nonetheless. The hips will tell you if they're going left, right, or straight. So, watch the hips of your opponents, and plan your response.

## It's A New Day

Just because something worked yesterday doesn't mean it's going to work today. I've said it before, not all tradition is good. Last year's effort will not win you this year's championship, I guarantee it my friends. Don't be afraid to start something new with your team when the old stuff just isn't cutting it. Seasons change, and the method that worked before might simply be outdated now. You know, they say that insanity is doing the same thing, expecting different results. What about doing the same thing, expecting the same failing results? Isn't that cray too?

Imagine trying to use the software from the iPhone 1 on the iPhone 8. Sure, it might actually turn on, but it's going to be a terrible response time. That's why I say that you can create what works for you as long as it's within the boundaries of your authority. We have too many leaders out there showing cowardice because they don't want to look stupid. Well, would you rather look dumb and win, or look dumb and lose when you could've won? Just asking. Don't be afraid to step out and step up to the challenge of creating something new if it's needed.

## Smiles Amplify Stupidity In Others

When I was in the police academy, I remember going through our combat techniques course. I had trained in martial arts for almost all of my life, and it helped to know a little more than what was being taught. On the other hand, I didn't know a lot about Brazilian Ju-Jitsu, and that is what we were working on in the mat room one particular day. Now, I've never prided myself in being some indestructible Kung Fu master, but I do know a few tricks. One day, I was in the mat room grappling with the lead instructor. He was one of those unassuming guys that looked like he should manage a grocery store, but he was just camouflaging the reality that he could fold you up like a pretzel at any time.

I don't remember how I ended up on my back, but nevertheless, there I was getting choked and punched in the face. All the while, he was literally whispering in my ear, "I'm gonna kill you!" Now, for the record, he didn't mean it folks, it was just a way to help us understand how multifaceted the stressors are that a first responder will face if you ever end up fighting for your life, or someone else's. Anyway, there I was getting my butt kicked, and not bragging, but I was definitely top three in grappling, and defensive tactics out of my academy class. He kept pounding away on me as I maintained my composure, controlled my breathing, and looked for weaknesses in his attack.

After a while, I was running out of options, and I found myself in an armbar, which is basically when someone manipulates the arm's natural direction of movement so that it's excruciatingly painful. I didn't even try to move because he had me. Then I noticed something. Every time he bent my arm, or locked me down in a painful manner, I laughed. I wasn't being disrespectful, but it's how I dealt with pain. Instead of crying or screaming, I would giggle and laugh. The first time it happened, he was puzzled. "Do you think this is a game Wilson?" he yelled at me. "No sir, it's just how I deal with pain sir," I told him. "Well, you better find another way to deal with it, cause you're gonna make somebody angry doing that," he told me. We continued fighting, and every time he pinned me or hurt me, I would laugh.

Then I realized that every time I laughed, he assumed he had me in a painful position. Up until that moment, he really did, but then I started strategizing. So, the next time he had me in a mildly painful position that I could still work out of, I began to laugh. He then held that weak position, thinking that I was going to surrender and tap. All of a sudden, "BOOM!" The next thing you know, I caught him with an elbow to the head, and had him pinned down to the mat. The old switch up, they say.

Another example would be Jack Johnson, the famous boxer. Johnson became the first black heavyweight world boxing champion, but in the height of the Jim Crow Era, this was absolutely abominable for the white race. So much so, that a former white champion named Jim Jeffries, came out of retirement to put Johnson in his place. They considered Jeffries, "The Great White Hope!" Their expectations were that Jeffries would beat Johnson into the ground and reclaim the world title for the white race. Well, it didn't turn out so good for Ol' Jeffries. It still wasn't an easy thing for Johnson to endure though.

"Porch Monkey, Slave, Black Dog...BOOOOO!" the ocean of white faces shouted as Johnson made his way to the ring. He never flinched though, they say, he only smiled. In the ring, Jeffries realized quickly that he was not the better of the two boxers. As Johnson etched his painful blows through the defensive position of Jeffries, he kept his composure and battled away. Then, Jeffries timed a punch perfectly and opened a cut on Johnson's face. Instead of shrinking back though, with blood on his face, and in his mouth...Johnson smiled! This infuriated Jeffries, now compromising his boxing focus because of his loss of emotional composure. It's said that every time Jeffries would fire forward, Johnson would weather the flurry, punch hard, and smile. After some time, smiling became the thing that beat

Jeffries the most. Although Johnson delivered a Class-A butt whooping, it was the smile that fatigued Jeffries the most. With every smile, came a burst of emotional reactions, until eventually he just tired himself out.

If you beat a man in his heart, and mind, everything else falls apart on its own. What I learned about Johnson though was this, he had planned it all along. He knew what kind of external opposition he was going to face, but the one thing he knew that could not be touched was his internal conversation. He knew that he was a bold man of faith, courage, and phenomenal boxing talent. So, he smiled to remind himself of who he was, and to let any naysayers know, they couldn't touch him. The more he smiled, the more enraged everybody else was, but that just let Johnson know that he was in control.

An African proverb says, "When there is no enemy within, the enemy without can do me no harm!" Do you smile in the face of your opposition, or do you cry? Do you fly off the handle, and make poor decisions? Or, do you plan to smile anyway because you know that in the end, you will win? You know, the bible even says to love your enemies. In doing so, you put hot coals on their heads, because as much as they hate you, they can't extinguish your composure and compassion. It's all strategy.

## **He's Getting Mad**

I remember the first time I saw Sylvester Stallone play the classic character Rocky. One of my favorite movies with that character was when he fought the Russian boxer Drago, played by Dolph Lundgren. Man, what a battle it turned out to be. If you didn't imagine yourself training with Sly in the winter cold, you didn't watch it, ha-ha. After Apollo Creed died, Rocky swore to avenge his death, and decided to fight in the steroid enhanced boxer's home country of Russia.

During the fight, Rocky was taking a serious beating. To the point where his trainers almost threw in the towel, signifying that the fight was over and he was sustaining too much damage. Rocky, on the other hand refused. Instead of moving out of the way, he stepped into the giant Russian's reach. With every blow that he took, he would wobble back to his feet, and begin to taunt the Russian while throwing response shots himself. The Russian simply could not understand how he was taking so much damage, let alone, why? Even his trainers began to yell and scream, wondering what he was doing.

As one of his corner men yelled for him to move, the other corner man told him not to. The one trainer said, "He's getting killed out there." And the other trainer responded, "No, he's getting mad." It was all in Rocky's strategy. While it was a painful strategy, it was effective. Naturally, the more muscle a person has, the more oxygen it requires to fuel those large arms. Rocky was causing the big Russian's cardiovascular system to be tested to the point that even his steroids could not help him. After taking enough shots, Rocky returned the favor, and began to beat the Russian into submission until ultimately, he KO'd Drago.

Sometimes, as a leader you will have to resort to an unorthodox and seemingly unfavorable strategy to win. Not everything has to be understood by everyone else as long as you have a clear understanding of why you're doing what you're doing. And, most of all, if they can yield the results that you want. Rocky knew that he was able to take the beating because he was going to give a beating right back. You have to know as the leader of your team, what to do, and when to do it even in the midst of being told, 'No,' at times. This does not mean you become overconfident and cocky, throwing complete common sense to the wind. But, it doesn't mean that you can't step back and launch your own creative attack if you know that it will work in the end. As a leader, don't be afraid to do what everyone else says you should not do, if they are not willing to get into the ring and suffer with you. As long as you are not putting other people in harm's way, then I say, 'Go after it.'

## *Free Game*

One of the best strategies for success in anything that you do...is to do it! See what you want, count the cost, determine how much you're willing to pay, and then dominate.

### **Strategy Smarts**

Problems are a matter of perspective in every way, shape, form and fashion. The issue that most people have is that they see the problem as something that cannot be solved, which is the absolute opposite of the definition. A problem, inherently, is something that requires solving or breaking down. Leadership is no different. Strategy, in the case of leadership, is always a matter of perspective and insight. The better you know your adversary, the better the solutions you have.

The reason the Roman armies were so superior during their time, was because they understood their adversaries and opponents. Even in the simplest terms, they understood that if they had enough people, no matter how strong their opponent might be, they would eventually wear out their resources and make their enemy's numbers count for nothing. This again, is a matter of strategy. One of the worst strategies I have ever seen was during the old days, when armies would literally line their men up across a battlefield and fire at each other. Their strategy was plainly to have more human bodies to sacrifice than the opposing force had bullets. This of course was an absolutely horrible idea that cost many willing souls their lives because of poor war strategy. The most interesting part was seeing rudimentary and outdated battle tactics come up against something like a sharpshooter or sniper. The element of surprise is always a plus, no matter what you're doing.

If you are doing the same thing, and expecting different outcomes, you're wasting your time. Why not take advantage of people's traditional expectations? The curve ball was a pain in the butt for batters, because they expected a fast ball or straight pitch down the center. It's the element of surprise that wins big. It's the same in your profession, schoolwork, or even your family for that matter. What areas can you turn upside down and pull the shock factor out? Where can you mix things up when everyone and everything is laying low? Where can you be a sniper when your challenges line up straight across the field from you?

Imagine being lined up one by one across a field and suddenly you see the person next to you fall. Then, three men down, another soldier hits the ground, and then another, and another until everyone breaks rank and begins to scramble because some unknown force is dropping them one by one. Think of the panic that would set in, only to find out later that one man in a tree across the field with a sniper rifle picked off half of your troop without even being seen or heard. Who has the better strategy here? In the same way, for leaders, you have to study your opponent and know what you're up against so that you can direct your team in the best manner. Don't set them up for failure by being slack and lazy. That is the equivalent of lining them up across a battlefield and allowing your adversary to take three shots at each man. That is stupid. Take the time to research and understand what you're fighting, and from there, rooted in purpose, vision, commitment and ownership, you can devise something that will literally shut down a game. Strategy is not a matter of who is the strongest, strategy is a matter of who is the smartest. But even the word smart doesn't mean that you need a secondary college degree. Being smart means that you've taken the time to break through the surface level of knowledge, and attain something useful that will give you the upper hand.

When you think about the Navy SEALs, most people look at them as unbreakable commando superhuman men. If you've ever watched a documentary on their training, you would notice that they are ordinary men with extraordinary resilience. I remember watching one of the classes go through their training on television one day. The very last week of their training is called "Hell Week." And from what I could see, it was just that. I was captivated by the fact that these extraordinary military men from all different branches were coming in and quitting. Most classes were starting with over 100 soldiers.

I'm not talking about retail store clerks, I'm talking Green Beret's, Army Rangers, Recon Specialists, Coast Guard Special Teams, and a host of others. Yet, at times only 12 or 13 would graduate. That says something about the process and strategy used in picking out the best suited recruits. One of the exercises was for the men to take one deep breath, jump into a 12 or 14ft pool, do a somersault underwater, and then swim to the other side and back on that one breath with no push off from the wall. If you have ever swam in a pool, or had a little bit of underwater fun, you understand just how difficult that is. Especially since you're talking about a 50-yard swim.

As you can imagine, with carbon dioxide building up in the lungs, and the weight of exhaustion on top of added mental challenges, that particular event was horrible. I watched more than half of the men swim down and back underwater, and just as they touched the wall, they blacked out. You heard it right, they stopped breathing underwater. Now, there were definitely instructors with air tanks waiting to push them up and bring them back to life, but still...come on. These men swam down and back, and absolutely refused to come up for air even though they understood the cost.

This exercise is a test of so many things simultaneously, but it was also a strategy. The great Dr. Eric Thomas, or as some of you may know him, "E.T. The Hip Hop Preacher" said, that when you want to succeed as bad as you want to breathe, then you'll be successful." These men took it a step further in my book. They refused to breathe, because they wanted to succeed so bad. Navy SEALs go into the hardest places in the world and face dangers that we know nothing about, for that very reason. If there was a modern-day military ninja, Navy SEALs would be it. Back to the example though.

The men would be pushed out of the pool by the instructors from the water. Almost lifeless bodies would scrape against the concrete pool siding and flop onto the cement floor, just as the waiting instructors would begin CPR and pump the water out of their lungs to get them breathing again. Sounds like a good time, right? To them, the instructor that is, it was no big deal. Why though? Because they had been there before, they knew that it was possible to make it out and continue on. One of the instructors was asked, "Why in the world they would put their trainees into a position where they could possibly die?" The answer was both astonishing, and easily understood. He said, "Navy SEALs understand that every mission they take could cost them their life. If they are not willing to give their life in a pool, they will not be willing to give their life on a mission if it requires it. If they aren't afraid of death now, death will not scare them ever again."

Those are the men that we want to have our backs in the middle of a heated battle. Men that aren't afraid to go to the very edge of life and back. If they aren't willing to do what's necessary in a controlled environment, they will fall apart in an uncontrolled and chaotic storm. They're weeding out process is all part of their strategy on developing the very best military leaders the world has to offer, US Navy SEALs. They are literally shielding the country from poor performance by developing such a hard charging strategy that would only allow the best of the best to make it through. It isn't the man's ability to fight that they are testing as much as it is their ability to shield others even if it cost everything they have. Once again, the epitome of Shield Over Spear.

## *Free Game*

Having a motto that you can live by will help you develop strategies to achieve success in different parts of your life. You need a statement locked in your heart to keep you moving when the world slows down around you.

## **8 Mile Message**

One of the greatest cinematic strategies in my opinion took place in the movie, "8 Mile." In the film, the celebrity rapper, Eminem, plays the character, "Jimmy Smith", who also goes by the name, "B-Rabbit." As in, Bunny Rabbit, because he's pretty fair skinned, ha-ha. He grew up in Detroit, Michigan, and not on the good side of the train tracks, literally. Everything around him involved struggle, poverty, abuse, lack, hopelessness, violence, and the likes. B-Rabbit hung out with a group that spent most of their time beating the streets, or in the middle of the hottest battle rap location in the city, "The Shelter!"

In the movie, B-Rabbit is a great freestyle rapper just trying to catch a break and move out of 8 Mile. For him, working or rapping is the only way to escape. He ends up at 'The Shelter' towards the end of the picture, and battle raps against a group called, "Free World." This group is led by a well-known rapper, "Papa Doc," being played by the well-known actor from "The Avengers," Anthony Mackie. Here's where it gets interesting. B-Rabbit has found a way to dismantle all of the opposing group's rappers, one by one. Then, it was time for 'Papa Doc.' B-Rabbit lost the coin toss and had to go first, but he was prepared. Goodness gracious...he was prepared. He smirks for a minute and then steps to the edge of the stage, raising his hand in the air, he says, "Now everybody from the 3-1-3, put your hands up and rock with me!'

The entire room erupts into a unified sway as hands flow up and down in a synchronized rhythm. And then the slaughter begins! B-Rabbit turns to Papa Doc and says, "Now while he stands tough, notice that this man did not have his hands up." At this point, he's bringing attention to the fact that as much as Papa Doc claims to be the king of the 8 Mile area, he wasn't even really from there. B-Rabbit goes on a rampage with cut downs, and then he puts the nail in the coffin, as one might say. But, he does something unconventional and totally unexpected. He turns his attention, to himself.

You see, in the battle rap arena, the whole purpose is to display your lyricism and ability to shut down, and embarrass the other rapper. So, cuts downs are the name of the game. B-Rabbit's strategy though was full proof. He starts by addressing the faults in his friends, then relationship, and financial issues. He goes on to bring light to the fact that he didn't come from the greatest of places, but never gave up and pressed on. After using his life as an example, he turns the heat back on to Papa Doc.

As he closes out, he says something to Papa Doc that literally made him speechless. He said, "Here, tell these people something they don't know about me," and tosses the microphone to Papa Doc. He steps back towards his friends, as Papa Doc can't even formulate a thought. He had just taken every piece of material that Papa Doc was going to use. Imagine an old western, where two-gun slingers were going to meet in the middle of the street at high noon for a duel. Now imagine one of the shooters walking over to his opponent, taking his gun out of the holster, emptying all of the bullets onto the ground, and placing an empty gun back in its place before returning to his spot in the road. Then, the bell rings and naturally, one shooter loses...the one with the empty gun. That is literally what B-Rabbit did. He took all of Papa Doc's ammunition, used it against him, and left anything he couldn't use on the ground for everybody else to see. Talk about a strategy.

Now, let's break it down. In leadership, we all have insecurities and shortcomings. The issue is, seldom do we see leaders incorporate those things into their success strategy. No, instead, they hide them. What if your classmate came in one day and said, "Hey, I know I'm the group leader, but if we're going to succeed, I need you to know the areas that I'm not strong in so that you can help me"? What if that happened? How would that team respond knowing that their leader was confident only in his/her ability to master their strengths and delegate the assignments to other strong teammates that are masters of the areas he/she is weak in? Can you imagine a team like that?

That, my friends, is a serious strategy that involves self-awareness, inclusion, transparency, focus, and trust. B-Rabbit simply utilized his weaknesses as strengths. I would recommend that you do the same with the teams that you are leading, or just yourself. What are those things you are able to call out about yourself, so that nobody else has to call it out in a derogatory manner? It's better to bring your own truth into the light, than to have someone else drag it out of the dark by force.

In this example, you shield yourself with truth, and foreknowledge. B-Rabbit knew his life story, and he knew that Papa Doc was going to attack that story. So, he didn't wait. He developed an on the spot strategy that utilized those very things to make him rap king of "The Shelter." That's difficult for people to do because of ego. What about you? We all know that it's one thing if you talk about, or joke with your siblings or friends. It's another thing when somebody else tries to embarrass or downplay their significance. B-Rabbit shielded his friends from Papa Doc's ridicule by taking the sharpness off his strikes. His friends knew that he had their best interest at heart, and that what he was saying wasn't meant to tear them down. It was just one more reason for them to trust him. They knew that being friends with B-Rabbit meant that they were going to be attacked also, but Rabbit used his words as a shield, and then Papa Doc's story as a spear against him. It was one heck of a battle, and one heck of a strategy.

In what areas of your life can you utilize some setbacks to help you move forward? What things have you tried to hide that would benefit you to bring out into the light? Remember, before an arrow can be launched, it must be pulled back first.

Remember, an arrow cannot be launched from a bow unless it is first pulled back and then released. What's going to launch you?

## *Free Game*

One of the most powerfully strategic weapons that you have in your hand is honesty. If you want to apply the shield and the spear simultaneously, be honest. When there is no deceit present, the allies of darkness can find no agreement. What I mean is that when you're having a bad day, thinking about something unfavorable, or desiring something that isn't the best for you, you will always find a co-signer. When you're upset, there is always somebody or something that will help validate your feelings and egg you on to do what you want to do. When you're honest though, I mean to the core, you know what must be done. As a great leader, I expect you to do what's right.

### **Shield Over Spear Chapter Summary**

The old saying goes, "If you fail to plan, you plan to fail." I'm not sure who said it first, but it's a significant statement nonetheless. As we discussed earlier, it's not always a matter of who's the strongest, as much as it is about who's the smartest. Leaders know how to make the most of situations, no matter what the situation may be. Strategy is an important weapon that leaders must utilize in order to accomplish a desired goal. Having a vision is not enough. Strategy is the gasoline that keeps the battle raging, but action is what brings about results.

# Principle 6: Action

*The only impossible journey, is the one you never begin!*

*-Tony Robbins*

## **Action, is a thing done!**

After many days of battle, the Spartan numbers had dwindled greatly. The king, Xerxes, sent emissaries to speak with Leonidas. "Leonidas, you have fought hard, and the mighty Xerxes has seen it. You want power? Xerxes will make you the most powerful king in Greece. You want land? You will be ruler of all things Greek. All you must do is drop your weapons, and kneel to Xerxes," the messenger said. King Leonidas stood with his shoulders high, and a fearless scowl on his face. Then it happened. He dropped his spear, and with all of our hearts breaking as movie watchers, Leonidas dropped to his knees, and bowed to Xerxes. The Persian king lifted his arms in victory from atop his royal carriage. As Leonidas glared at the ground, memories passed through his mind. He closed his eyes, and envisioned his wife's face, his boy, his soldiers, and his city...Sparta.

His eyes opened and squinted as his mouth balled up and the feeling of fire raged from within. He inhaled! "Stelios!!!" he roared. Immediately, the Spartan formation broke open as Stelios, the fearless soldier ran forward. With spear in hand, in just a few strides, he stepped on King Leonidas' back and launched into the air. Descending on the Persian messenger, he pressed the tip of his spear through the chest of the enemy opposition before landing on his feet and into a defensive position. In the face of overwhelming forces, and unmeasurable odds, they attacked...they took massive action!

With just a quarter of their original numbers still alive, they attacked. They did not run away; they ran forward with all of their strength. Can you believe it? Imagine a football team lining up on the field with the typical number of players, only to look up and see the opposing side bringing their entire team on to the field. And then, the mere 11 or 12 players yell...ATTACK! Can you picture that? I love it. The guts to be bold, disciplined and yet reckless. For Spartans, there was no giving up, there was no sitting back, there was no such thing as kneeling, and there was no surrender! Act and attack! What about you?

## A Common Mistake

This is a message you should never forget. The fact that you're always busy does not mean you're being productive, and making progress. A lot of people assume that because they have a lot going on in their life, they're taking action. Not necessarily. Action, for a leader, means that every step you take towards accomplishing the mission makes you better. There are tons of people out there running around, doing absolutely nothing productive.

Though I'm not very good at it, I admire the game of chess. It's a matter of strategy, and action. You have to watch the action steps of your opponent, while still having a game plan for yourself. It's actually quite crazy when you think about it. The lowest ranking figure has the power to be elevated in rank, and take the power of your opponent's king or queen. In that game, just like in leadership, you can't just toss your pieces anywhere.

Once you have your strategy in place, you commit to it, and fight until the strategy succeeds or needs to be updated, either way, you take action. A lot of authoritative figures are really good at delegating things, but never taking the initiative to make sure it's worth delegating in the first place. If more leaders took the time to measure the return factor versus the time utilized, I think we'd find ourselves at a better place more often.

The biggest take away here is this. BE PRODUCTIVE WHILE TAKING ACTION! You don't have to solve every problem at once, but you can keep the flow going. Don't get stuck doing stupid stuff, and calling it progress.

## **The Immortals**

The immortals, that's what they were called. The king was told of this group of special forces Persian warriors. It's because the legend surrounding them said that they could not be killed. It seemed as if every time one of them fell in battle, there was one more standing right back in their place, as if the fallen soldier had never fallen at all. When the mighty Spartan king heard of these, so called immortals, he had one thing to say, "Immortals? We'll put their names to the test."

The king was bold, brutal, and unwilling to be moved. He was a man of action. And, sure enough, as the immortals took their place on the field of battle, just like every other Persian soldier until that time, they fell also. Once the Spartans saw one bleed and die, the immortals had lost all of their credibility. The Spartans were not men of fear, they were men of pursuit and instruction. The king gave them one task, and one task only...Dominate!

What about your leadership style? How many times have you fallen short because you believed a story that someone told you about a situation you were facing? How many times have you looked at an obstacle or challenge and said to yourself, "Because they couldn't do it, surely I can't do it either?" What thing have you allowed to take the place of the immortals? And most of all, are you ready to do what the Spartans did? Are you ready to apply pressure and meet your issue with the tip of your spear?

In this case, the immortals symbolize anything that can cause you to be afraid and overwhelmed by what you have heard and not yet experienced. It is a common tactic and strategy even in times where there is no physical person on the opposing side. For example, the first time I competed in a triathlon I was terrified. I wasn't afraid of the competition though; it was the water. I had never been in open water before. If you've ever done it, you know that a lake or ocean is nothing like a swimming pool. I had to get over all of the horror stories I had heard though, dial in, and run my race. I did just that. I told myself, "You better cut the crap and FIND A WAY...TO FIND THE WAY!" My immortals were beatable the moment I decided they were. So... FIND A WAY! Take action.

Additionally, remember that all of your emotions originate within you. I'll repeat that for the people in the back! All of your emotions originate within your own mind and heart. It drives me nuts when people say ridiculous stuff like, "They made me do it." Nobody made you do anything. If I say, "You're stupid," it's up to you to feel sad. It's the way that you interpreted what I said, not the words that came out of my mouth. You based your value on a relationship that holds no weight, and a statement that bears no truth. Stop blaming everybody else.

Action, that very phrase speaks volumes. Take action. What I am urging you to do is to violently and forcibly pull something into your possession so that you can utilize it to achieve a goal or end. Taking, does not require asking, nor permission. It is a matter of sheer will and power. Action is a step that breaks the boundaries of immobility. If you are going to take action, you will have to force something off the ground and in the direction that you choose. Find that thing, whatever it may be, and impose your will. This does not mean that you attempt to dominate people, that is the worst form of leadership. Honestly, it's not leadership at all. It's just an abuse of authority, rather than leadership at all. Remember, shield before the spear, not spear before shield.

## The Cause Of The Pause

What keeps people from acting, in one way or another, is fear. I should know, I wrote another book about it. No, seriously...go read the book. It's called, "Cornered By Fear: A Guide To Finding Your Freedom In The Fight!" It's on Amazon, or you can just email me at KD@Iamkdwilson.com, and I'll sign it and mail it to you at a discounted rate. But, fear is paralyzing. It makes you think it has more resources than it really does, that it's stronger than it really is, and can get to you whenever it desires.

Well, fear is full of, "Oops," almost slipped up, ha-ha. Fear is a liar, but remember, you have to believe the lie before it can have any power over you. You have to be in agreement with whatever is being said, or seen, before there can be any transference of control. So, if you find yourself freezing up all the time when the moment requires action, ask yourself these questions.

What am I afraid of?

_____

_____

_____

Why am I afraid of it?

_____

What will happen if this fear comes to pass?

---
---

Can I recover from it, if what I am afraid of comes true?

---
---

Can I get up and try again afterwards if I fail at this attempt?

---
---

People are afraid to be afraid. Everybody wants the payoff, but nobody wants the pain. If you're going to be a leader in anything that you do, you have to be willing to feel some pain. Pain is a part of the process, and the process is generated by action. When everything hits the fan, look for the calm one in the corner still sipping their drink, and casually stretching. That, is a person of action. They understand that stress is just a part of the journey that comes along with taking the fight to your opponent, whatever it may be. You heard me! Take the fight to their door step.

That means whatever you're having a problem with, you become the problem for the problem. And, if you're having a hard time figuring out who your opposition is, just think about anything that's trying to stop you, or hinder the success of you or your program. That is your opponent. Sometimes you are your worst adversary. So, make sure that in the end, you're not getting in your own way of seeing the results you've worked so hard for.

## Be In Place Or Be Replaced

When a person in leadership refuses to act, another must take their place. I'm reminded of the biblical story of David and Goliath. There was a young man named David that tended to his father Jesse's flock. David was a faithful, and a faith filled man. He always strived to do what was right, especially in regards to his love for God. David's brothers had gone off to war with King Saul to fight against the Philistines. David, being obedient and in place, stayed and tended to the flock. His father called him in one day. "David, take these goods to your brothers, and bring me news of how things are going with them," he said. So, David did just that. But, before he left to see his brothers, he found someone to take his place with the sheep. That's solid.

How many times do we just leave our place open as leaders? You know, when we assume everything will just magically be alright. That mentality of, "Oh it'll be ok." David didn't do that though. He knew that until he relinquished his position, he was responsible. Even in his absence, he left a shield in place. You have to do the same thing with your team and your role. If something should arise, taking action, and not just leaving your post, is critical.

This could be just as much a mental thing than physical. How many times have you just mentally checked out on your team, classmates, or even yourself? When you mentally check out, you are abandoning your post. Remember, it's easier to put together a plan, than it is to fix a big mess.

A few simple things you could do as a leader:

- Look for those people that have an understanding of your role and have them on standby.
- Have a strategy in place beforehand.
- Think ahead so that you're not caught off guard when challenges come your way.
- Don't abandon your post, mentally or physically, without having the next step thought out.

After David had filled his spot, he continued on to see his brothers. As he neared the camp, he saw the men rallied and on guard, but from a distance. The men were withdrawn from their normal battle positions. Then David learned why. A massive man, named Goliath stepped forward and began to challenge God and his army. David, being the man that he was, would not stand for it. He jolted forward, ready to fight, but was told to stand down. "David, that's Goliath, nobody can beat him," they said. David knew the power of position though, so he went to the king and asked for permission to fight the giant. The king allowed it, and David took to the field, and killed Goliath.

Not long after he killed the giant, David was made king over Saul. None of that would have happened if he wasn't actively in position though. They wouldn't have been able to find him on the day when the prophet came, but David was demonstrating commitment. I'm convinced that some of us aren't where we are supposed to be in life because we are out of place. We are out of place in our minds, hearts, and attitudes too often. We simply surrender control to our problems and lock up, like the army did when Goliath challenged them. I'm challenging you to be more like David, a man of integrity, and a man of action. King Saul was the man in charge when David showed up on the battlefield, but he was afraid to act like a king. David showed up, and in faith, mixed with training, he dropped the giant. When they got back home from battle, the people recognized the man of action, not the man with an attitude. They yelled, "Saul has killed thousands, but David has killed ten thousand." Recognition of one willing to step into place while others freeze is easy.

Action takes place when a need is seen and ability is present. Even when you break down the word, responsibility, it simply says that you have the 'ability' to 'respond'. It's all action, but if you lock up in the middle of a battle, or at the slightest sign of discomfort, you will be a poor leader all of your life. Take action!

## *Free Game*

Eagles fly high because it's what they do, and it's who they are. Chickens only fly temporarily when they are scared. If you find yourself jumping in panic when things startle you or don't go your way, you're acting like a chicken. Be calm, confident, and ride on the winds that try to push you off balance in life. Be the eagle you were created to be.

### **Living Sacrifice**

There is nothing more heroic or amazing that a human being can do, than to lay their life down for another. In one particular military branch, their motto is, "So that others may live!" Think about that for a minute, and all that it's saying. It doesn't mean that the people joining this branch of the military want to die, but it does say that they are willing to give the ultimate gift so that others may keep it. Wow! You know it reminds me of a movie, based on a true story. Naturally, it's a war movie. Sorry, ha-ha. It was about a Marine Corp unit overseas that had found themselves in a serious gunfight. In the movie, and in the true recollection of the incident, the Marines were battling against some determined terrorists that simply would not give up.

Shell casings were flying everywhere as the Marine troop moved through this urban battlefield. Unaware of where the enemy would attack from next, they worked their way through a small city and into a building. Hoping to have a few moments of concealment and cover, the men worked their way through the structure.

Unfortunately, there was no time to rest, as the opposing forces followed them into the abandon building. In a matter of minutes, with little sunlight and the weight of war bearing down on them, shots rang out again. There was no time to gather thoughts, only targets. The fight was so much worse this time because there was a full-on gunfight in a small building that provided very little room to move around in. "Contact Right...Contact Right!" one Marine yelled, notifying others that hostiles were attacking from a certain direction.

Bullet after bullet, shot after shot, the small building had become a warzone. After some time had passed, the terrorist attackers realized they were taking a beating, and wouldn't win the fight. As a matter of fact, there were maybe two of them left, and then there were none. The Marines were exhausted, and some had injuries from the gunfight as they moved through and out of the building. All of a sudden, something heavy hit the floor and bounced in front of them. One of the downed terrorist fighters on the second level above them had dropped a grenade over the side, as he took his last breath. "GRENADE!" one Marine yelled!

But, the Marine closest to it didn't yell at all. No! This loving, caring, father, brother, uncle, warrior, and friend did what most wouldn't even consider, but wasn't even a second thought for him. This man! Somebody's boy! Somebody's husband and dad, did the most that any leader could ever do. This hero threw his body on the grenade to save his brothers.

He didn't say a word, because he was a man of action. The explosion alone could have blown a hole in the side of a building. That's the power of a grenade. He curled his body over it, and took all of the pain for his friends. Sadly, his Kevlar vest and gear weren't enough to save him. He died in that building...so that others could live. The Marines scrambled to patch his wounds, perform CPR, and evacuate him to a nearby base, but it was too late. "So that OTHERS may live," another military branch stated! "The few...and the proud," the Marine motto goes. On that day, that leader of a warrior, covered them all. He didn't talk about it though, he lived as a man of action.

What does that mean to you? What does it mean to be a leader of action?

_____
_____
_____
_____
_____

When have you taken action when others froze? And why?

_____

What would your life be like if you talked less about what you were going to do, and just did it?

If you are slow to respond when you know you should, what will it take to get you moving?

What are some of the things that have hindered you in that area of taking action? (Friendships, Excuses...Etc.)

Know this, we will always be limited and imprisoned by hesitation when fear is our most dominant emotion. In order to avoid hesitating when something valuable is on the line, for yourself, or your team, here's a few things to consider:

- What will happen if you don't act?
- How many people are counting on you?
- How much can be gained in your successful action?
- How awesome will you feel when somebody says, "Because of your actions, we won"?

If you're going to lift a shield of action over your team, you have to become a leader that sees your own ability to respond. Responsibility is not complex. We look at it as a negative most days, because we fear being held accountable. It's just the 'ability,' to respond. From there, you just make the decision to do so. Responsibility, coupled with the heart to sacrifice, and the will to win, opens up an avenue for success like you'd never believe.

## *Free Game*

If your team is afraid to act, even though they have the ability to do so, give them something to believe in.

### **Shield Over Spear Chapter Summary**

What is awareness without action? A waste, that's what it is. "Hey, that baby is about to fall into that pool," she yelled, but never moved. Imagine the baby falling in the water and drowning. What would you say to the woman that was within reaching distance, but was too afraid to lose her beach chair at the pool? You'd throw a fit, that's what you'd do. You would tell her that she could've saved the child, and that she should be ashamed. What if she said, "It wasn't my child though?" How would you respond? You would probably tell her that you didn't care whose child it was, she was the one that saw it, and should have acted.

Question! How many times has that been you? How many times have you seen somebody in need of a hero, and you just sat there because it wasn't quite your problem? Were you ashamed of yourself? Probably not, but you should be. If you saw a need that you felt compelled to respond to, and didn't...now is your chance for a redo. You know someone once said, "The richest place in the world is the graveyard." The graveyard is where all of the cures for disease, solutions to poverty, increase in education and so much more was put to rest. Why though? The graveyard is full of living dreams trapped in dead places. The people that were responsible for them most likely had a plan and a purpose, but they never took action. They probably sat on their hopes while wishing that a shooting star would pass them by. As a leader, let me tell you something...there are no shooting stars for you! There is no magic pill, no one night fix, no cheat code and no short cut. For you, as a leader, there is fear, but still movement. You may lack, but you still have a heart to give. All of your hard work will boil down to this sixth element of action that shields you from regret, and launches you into the fullness of your much-earned results.

# Principle 7: Results

*No matter what, find a way...to find the way!*

*-K.D. Wilson*

## **RESULTS, are simply the consequences and outcome of action.**

He knew that he wasn't coming back home. The king knew that none of them were ever coming back. As they marched away from Sparta, the king told the congressmen, "Sparta will need sons!" What was he saying? The obvious...that they were ready, willing, and expecting to shield. They were undoubtedly dedicated to the fact that the greatest shield they carried, was their own life. They would not surrender their shields. They would not have their shields taken, but they would lay them down so that others may cross over on their actions as the bridge leading to their independence if need be.

Now, some may say...to gain what? Any leader would know the answer to that. FREEDOM! But, if you saw the movie, you would know that the results of that battle, while not yielding the fullness of their anticipations, did bring about hope! As a leader, and as a person, three things reign supreme. These things are Faith, Hope, and Love! All of which the king and his men showed, and lived when it came to their families, country, and brothers. Faith, Hope, and Love! With those three components, your results, as a leader will always win over anything else!

## **Hold The Line**

A great rule to remember when it comes to leadership and results is this, "Never change your vision to accommodate your chaos." I recall almost giving up on love. That sounds like a sappy thing to say I'm sure, but I'm not joking at all. Once, I was dating this young lady who was well known and loved by all of our school peers. Me, being the average nice guy, was just happy to be in her presence. I remember taking her car one time, she let me, I didn't steal it ha-ha. Anyway, I took her car, and put poster boards in all of the windows facing out. When you walked past the car, you would read each of our dates, and locations on them. In the driver seat, I placed a teddy bear with a thin chain and my birthstone around its neck. Naturally, I was assuming that the results of such an amazing Valentines gift would yield great return. Not in the way that most of you are thinking, just in the sense of great appreciation and a deeper connection.

But, as she came out to the parking lot and saw her car, her response was breathtaking, and not in a good way. "Oh," she said, "That's nice." You can imagine the shock and somewhat bewilderment that I was experiencing after having gone through so much and done so much work, only to be given a mediocre response. But, that wasn't her fault, it was my expectations. Remember, all of your feelings come from you! As a leader, you have to guard yourself against building up permanent walls due to temporary setbacks. In my case, after our relationship ended, I couldn't have cared less about being someone's boyfriend. I didn't mind being on my own. Because of the frustration and pain that I experienced, I assumed that isolation was the best method. I was wrong, and I would once again charge you not to make the same mistake that I almost did. Make sure, that no matter what, you readjust your strategy and your line of sight but not your purpose, character, and heart.

So many people quit when they don't get the automatic results that they want or hoped for. Comparison is a big issue when it comes to this particular place. When you look at yourself and then compare your results to that of someone else, you're already doing yourself a disservice. No matter what you do, nor the role that you were in, you are not them, and they are not you. Be authentically who you are, and work your butt off to get what you need in life.

Have you ever allowed someone else's response to dictate and control what you believed or how you felt about a thing? If so, why? If not, how did you find that balance?

___

___

What advice would you give to someone that really allows other people to control their actions?

___

___

How do you help friends and teammates work through the insecurities of unwelcomed results?

___

___

## **The Formula**

One way or another...purpose, vision, commitment, ownership, strategy, and action will produce results. Every action has an equal or opposite reaction, we all learned that in school. But, patience is key. You have so many people that have only put three hours of thought into something, and they want to write a book. They have done one bodybuilding competition, and now they want to be a coach. They fix their air conditioning system at their house, and now they consider themselves an engineer. What I'm trying to say is that you shouldn't assume that you have all of the pieces to the puzzle just because you saw a picture. Be sure that you are not giving yourself too much credit for short wins. Take credit for what you have achieved and accomplished, but don't assume that your one day of results equals a lifetime of success.

Results will always reveal something new about you. I love retelling the story from a book that I read called, Extreme Ownership. In one chapter, the book talks about a Navy SEAL Academy exercise. In this particular exercise, different boat crews, one through six, had to get in their boats, paddle out into the ocean, flip the boat over, get everybody back inside and then paddle back to shore.

One particular boat crew leader found his team coming in last each time. On the opposite end, the first-place boat crew found themselves winning every evolution of the exercise, and totally dominating. The losing boat crew leader constantly griped and complained about his team and the poor results they were getting. He credited their loss to lack of effort and poor execution from those that were under his command. The winning boat crew leader accredited winning to the willing hearts of those under his command. As you can see, there is a drastic difference in both the results and the mindsets of the two boat crew leaders.

The senior chief grew tired of watching the losing boat crew leader complain. He called the winning boat crew leader and the losing boat crew leader into a huddle. He then swapped leaders between the winning and losing crews. The losing boat crew leader was ecstatic because he felt that he would now be able to show how great of a leader he was with capable and able bodies. The winning boat crew leader, while slightly frustrated, took ownership of the losing crew. During the next exercise evolution, the former losing boat crew had now crept their way up into second place right behind the dominating boat crew.

The interesting thing was, the former losing boat crew leader was struggling to keep up with the dominant boat crew's performance.

Now the losing boat crew leader, though in command, was the weakest link. By the time the next evolution had begun, the former losing boat crew was now in first place and dominating the former winning boat crew. When huddled back together, the former losing boat crew leader realized that it was his leadership all along that was causing the poor results, not the team's effort. Leadership is contagious, and automatically produces great results when a great leader is in the right position and has the right resources.

The winning boat crew leader took the losing boat crew and made them winners also. This happened all while the losing boat crew leader joined the previously winning boat crew and discovered just how weak he was himself. Sometimes we are not getting the results we want because we are failing to see that we are the problem. The blessing of it all is that problems can be solved, therefore so can your leadership style if what you're doing is proving to be a negative instead of a positive.

**Stepping Stones**

Hopefully you have noticed that this entire book has simply been my effort to lay down stepping stones for you to achieve a particular goal. When we started this journey, everything came down to the two most dominant principles in the book, which are purpose and results. If you understand your purpose, you can find a way to get the results that you want. If you don't understand that you have a purpose in doing what you're doing, you will settle for any results that you get, or assume that what you get is the best that you can achieve.

Take football for instance. It's one of those age-old American love affairs that is based on results. Whether it be in high school, college or the professional leagues, results matter the most. You can have a former Super Bowl champion coach that gets fired after the next two losing seasons. How? He failed to produce results. If you're going to be a legacy minded leader, you have to be able to reproduce the results that got you the job in the first place.

Great leaders, while experiencing the ups and downs of life, never forget where they came from. Those that forget where they started, don't appreciate where they are, and where they may one day be. If you are a team leader, whether it be in school, a church, or even just at home, you have to be able to reproduce. The greatest sign of a leader is their ability to reproduce after themselves. After all, you cannot be a leader if no one is willing to follow you.

The greatest tragedy though, is when the wrong people reproduce after themselves. That's not you though! No, you see the need to step in with character, integrity, and strong work ethic, because you know the value of them all. You know that leaders are the ones that make or break a team, and the only thing you're breaking is bad habits. You know that if, and when the results do show up, you didn't do it on your own. You know how to give other people credit for their contributions to the overall success of a project. That is why you need to reproduce after yourself in the area of leadership results. You are worth duplicating!

### *Free Game*

Sometimes we don't get the results we want because we're

expecting them to look a certain way. Don't be so locked in to your expectations. Instead, learn to discern when you've really succeeded in something, and when it's just a good feeling.

## Trap House

One major pit fall for many leaders and authoritative figures is becoming results oriented to the degree that you are willing to sacrifice your team and your honor. If you are so focused on getting the results you want that you're willing to abandon your character and break the bonds of relationship with those that you should be shielding, you are failing. Some people become addicted to results. After all, we do have a physiological response to them. When you experience fulfillment or excitement, you get a hit of dopamine. Dopamine is one of the brain's neurotransmitter's that releases a chemical into the body that helps regulate emotional responses. If it helps, and to explain the addictive nature of the dopamine/results intersection, think about drug addiction.

Do you know why people sometimes start with a cigarette, and end up on heroine? I know, I know...poor decisions. But, what else? It's the high, and the dopamine rush. Again, I'm not generalizing everybody that's every struggled with addictions, but you get the picture. Even if it's being used to mask fear, past trauma, sickness and such, it's still the high they're chasing. When you smoke a cigarette, nicotine, which typically helps calm the body, is introduced. When stress becomes too much, and a cigarette won't cut it, some people move up the drug chain. Marijuana is definitely a dopamine puller because dopamine makes you feel euphoric once the dominant chemical, ThC, is introduced to the body. Going even further, some people unfortunately take it to the extreme, and end up being slaves to major drugs like meth, cocaine, and heroine. Those are all massive dopamine users...thereby making it so addictive. But addiction isn't just about emotions, and internal battles.

For some, it's the spotlight that they value most. The intoxication of fame by way of previous results can cause one to become manipulative and lose who they are. I remember watching a documentary about a famous boxer. This particular Irish champion had been dominating his particular weight class, and finally came to America to fight in the states. He was definitely the favorite to win the fight, because he was known for never giving up and having a heart of steel. Little did he know, the individual that he would be fighting against did not share the same character that he did.

When the fight began, the favorite Irishman swarmed his opponent and began throwing bombs and precise shots causing the contender to buckle. The Irish boxer was flat out, living up to the hype. And then the tables turned drastically. After a round or two, the Irishman's opponent swung one time and connected right on the corner of his jaw. He collapsed and fell to the ground. This was something that had never happened to him. Everybody was shocked, particularly because his opponent was not known for his knockout power and strength. The Irish man was known for his unwillingness to fall, and now it had happened.

He got back to his feet, only to be hit with a flurry of punches in the face and ribs. His opponent swung, and one after the other, the Irishman's face began to swell, to the point where the fight had to be called for safety reasons. As his opponent came over to shake his hand and shake the hand of the Irishman's coach, who happened to be the Irish boxer's father, something unusual was discovered. When the Irishman's father shook the hand of his son's opponent, he realized that his gloves felt extremely thin. He held onto the boxer's hand and yelled for the referee and coaches to come over.

Once they did, they grabbed the boxer's wrist, refusing to let go so that he couldn't take the gloves off. Security then escorted him to the locker room. While the Irish boxer was no longer undefeated and being escorted to the hospital to treat his wounds, his opponent was being investigated in the locker room after the match. It was discovered that in the top of his gloves on both sides there were two small cuts. The cuts provided just enough space to pull the filling and padding out of it. That basically meant that the Irishman was hitting his opponent with padded gloves and his opponent was basically bareknuckle punching him in the face.

The opposing boxer's training crew denied any knowledge of the tampered glove incident, but they were all fired and charged criminally. As for the boxer, he was banned from boxing forever, and known as a cheater for the rest of his life. Unfortunately, the Irishman never recovered mentally and spiritually from the loss and beating that he took unfairly in the ring.

He resorted to isolation, and heavy drinking to mask and cope with his pain. It was to the degree that his wife had to take their children and leave because he was becoming hostile and dangerous. In a horrible turn of events, sometime later, the young Irish boxer took his life because he could not deal with his depression. The crushing blow of an unfair defeat pushed him over the edge. His death ultimately stemmed from a rigged match where someone valued fame, notoriety, and results more than integrity and their reputation.

Thankfully, that is not a normal thing that happens, death in that sense, I mean. But, it is not abnormal for people to cheat and do whatever they can to achieve what they want at any cost. Shield over spear is the absolute enemy of that concept. The whole purpose is to guard your integrity, character, and reputation by being the very best leader that you can be for those under your command and yourself. In doing so, you produce life and not death as it intersects with the journey that binds you to those you serve.

Sometimes people think they're failing at leadership, when in reality they simply don't have a system in place to gauge whether they're winning or losing. If you cannot measure your success, how will you know if you have attained it or not? Ultimately, everything comes down to systems. Strategy is most certainly your greatest help in this area, but I'm not talking about the production phase. I am referencing the system of response that you have, or do not have in place. For instance, if your team is not meeting a monthly quota, how are you keeping up with that information? And more so, what are you doing with the information you have that allows you to readjust your strategy and make the necessary changes in order for you to achieve the desired goal? Part of leadership is knowing when to hold and went to fold. You cannot rely on yesterday's tactics if you are trying to produce tomorrow's prize. So, how are you measuring your success rate or failure? That is something you need to know the answer to. And, if need be, reach out to someone that is producing or that operates in a position that you have been in.

## **Tangible Outcomes**

After Stelios broke rank and began the last attack that the mighty Spartan warriors unleashed, King Leonidas stepped forward. He did not bother to pick up his helmet, nor his shield.

This time, it was only about the spear! But why? I'll tell you why. Leonidas had spent his entire life growing in almost every area possible. He had shielded his family, soldiers and city as best as he could. The time had come for him to drop his shield, and heave his weapon of attack. There comes a time, when the shield must yield to the spear. When the attack is the only way to win. The king only wanted his trusty spear, it was the only thing he was after. He squinted his eyes to focus his vision, even as his brothers fell dead around him. He lunged forward with a mighty war cry and released the messenger of death into the air.

The spear traveled straight and far, as if it were shot like an arrow from the bow of a giant. Splitting air molecules in half, it traveled over the head of the Persian soldiers, straight towards king Xerxes. As the king stood with astonishment at the Spartans refusal to surrender, the Spear cut open the right cheek of the king's face. Seeing this, king Leonidas was satisfied to know that this so-called god king felt pain just like any other man.

Xerxes was terrified and moved to cover as Leonidas and the remaining soldiers were overwhelmed with arrows fired from their enemies. While some may say it was all a waste, the king knew that it was worth it. All of this came to be at the hands of leaders, all of the mighty men, that dared to put shield over spear!

**<u>Shield Over Spear Chapter Summary</u>**

While results are definitely what drives the person, the process is really what keeps you. The results only come about because someone is willing to endure what it takes to achieve what it is they are after. People don't miss the finish line because they aren't talented, gifted, or optimistic. People miss the finish line because they short changed the process that leads to the results they wanted. There is a reason that in the UFC (Ultimate Fighting Championship), rematches take place. Sometimes, fighters just get a fortunate shot, and drop their opponent. The question then becomes, "Was it just by chance, or training?" That's when the rematch gets scheduled.

Everybody has the same question, "Can they do it again?" At times, you do have those people that are one strike knockout fighters. Some of those fighters might be Anderson Silva, Amanda Nunes, Matt Hughes, Anthony Pettis, Connor McGregor, Frances Ngannou, and a host of others. When you have a rematch with fighters like them, you just earn the title of getting knocked out twice. It's the process and their power that made them great. If you're serious about getting the results that you want, make sure you master the first 6 principles. Make sure you don't take any short cuts. Make sure that when the time is right, you pick up your spear, and find out for yourself that everything has a weakness.

## The Finish

You know, the bible says, "There is no greater love than for one to lay down their life for another!" While you may never find yourself in that particular predicament, many have, and many chose to do just that. One of the most powerful relationships in the movie that exemplified indestructible leadership qualities was that of King Leonidas and Stelios! The amazing standard set in the lives of Spartan men came to life. Remember, Stelios was the ambitious soldier that yelled out to the king before they departed for the coast. He is the one that told the king that he was with him, to the death. Stelios, my friends, fulfilled his promise.

As the king fell to the ground after being struck with several arrows, his last moments neared. Grunting, and heaving for air, he glanced to his left. Stelios had taken a number of arrows to his chest and was fading quickly as well. But, not before saying one last thing! Even with death knocking at his door, Stelios mustered the strength to push closer to his bold leader. "My KING!" he said. "It is an honor, to die at your side!" And, never breaking the nature of his authentic self, Leonidas leaned quickly on his right arm. With a shifting movement, he lifted his left hand and grabbed that of his loyal friend, Stelios. In pain, and literally dying, he etched his name into the book of the world's greatest leaders and said, "It was an honor, to have lived...at yours!" Let the tears flow freely, my goodness. What love, and tribute to both men. Can someone say that about you? Is there anyone you can say that about? That it would be an honor to die by their side, and equally, to have lived at yours?

What took place there is what every true leader hopes for. They pray that they will be the type of person that other people just want to be around. The type of leader that demands excellence through example, and not explanation alone. The type of leader that deeply cares for the ones entrusted to their watch. I mean the leaders that others will happily fight for. The leaders that others would sacrifice for on their own account, and even die for. My friends, you can be that leader! This takes place when you see the need to be your best for others, and yourself. This comes to life when the 7 Indestructible Principles Of Success are burned into your psychology. Growth comes when you are ignited by PURPOSE, stabilized by VISION, characterized by COMMITMENT, honored by OWNERSHIP, progressing by STRATEGY, enlightened by ACTION, and empowered by RESULTS!

Stand tall on the battlefield of life, and in the end, you will reign victorious. Some will call you names, despise you, and judge you, but they will never extinguish your truth. You can do this! People will follow you into the fire, not because of your smarts alone, or your die-hard work ethic, but rather...the heart you have accepted as your own. It's the bravery needed to step out of your comfort zones, and into the unknown. It's the fight for the present, release of the past, and the courage...the courage to embrace tomorrow. You are not what you've come from. You are what's needed in this day and age. You will succeed, not because of the battles you've won on your own. My friend, it's the battles that you won by holding, "SHIELD OVER SPEAR!" Lead well my friends...lead well!

**Closing Note:**

Thank you so much for taking the time to read my second book. My prayer is that God would help you see the greatness He has destined you for. I pray that you would find freedom in who you are, and not for what you thought you needed to become. This book is for you...the champion. Despite your shortcomings and setbacks, you never gave up. Never Give Up! Please keep in touch, and by all means, share your testimonies and stories. You can contact me via the following:

Email: **KD@Iamkdwilson.com**

Instagram: Iamkdwilson

Twitter: Iam_kdwilson

Facebook: Iamkdwilson1

Website: **www.Iamkdwilson.com**

If you'd like to order my first book on overcoming fear, just email me. Any speaking inquires can be sent to the email address listed above. If you'd like books in bulk, you can also contact me via email and we will discuss discounted rates.

The day you were born, was the day that opportunity was placed into your hands. What you do with that opportunity in this lifetime, is up to you! Dominate with a full heart, and a fiery spirit!

-K.D. Wilson

Made in the USA
Columbia, SC
22 May 2023

16683123R00093